ADD AMS ANR ARN BCN
BKK BNE BOG BOM CAI C
CNW CPH DAM DCA DPS
FOC FRA HAM HAV HDD H
HND HNL HRE IAD JFK JK
LAX LGA LGW LHR LTN M
NAS NCE NRT NUE ORD O
PSY PTY PVG QND RAB SA
SKD STN SYD SZG TBS TI
WAW YBA YHZ YYZ

AVIOPOLIS
A BOOK ABOUT AIRPORTS

GILLIAN FULLER AND ROSS HARLEY

Black Dog Publishing Limited

Five things about airports

Airports and other networks are flow machines. They are designed to process the mass movement of people, equipment, things and concepts between land and air.

Airports are nodes in a global network of travel, trade, architecture, design, technological innovation, security, and more. They are part of a global 'city of bits'.

Airports synchronise with each other and other networks through global systems of regulation.

Airports signify the rise in a new type of urban form – 'metastable forms', which are constantly changing, yet appear stable.

Air traffic is increasing. Despite SARS, the events of September 11 and the 'war on terror', volumes of passenger and freight traffic have grown in 2004 by 5.9 per cent and 7.2 per cent, respectively.*

*source: IATA International Traffic Statistics: January 2004. This statistic signals a bounce back from the lulls in 2002 and 2003.

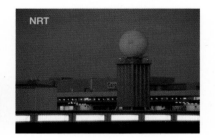

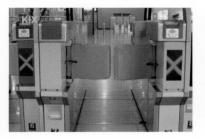

Contents

AMS

EVERY YEAR, ONE AND A HALF BILLION PASSENGERS MOVE THROUGH AIRPORTS. THEY ARE SCANNED, CHECKED AND UPLOADED INTO THE FLYING MACHINES THAT WILL TAKE THEM ON A HIGH-SPEED JOURNEY TO ELSEWHERE. AVIOPOLIS IS ABOUT HOW THIS NEW TYPE OF LIFE IN THE AIR IS CHANGING EVERYTHING ON THE GROUND.

Airports are a type of city designed to facilitate global mass-movement as efficiently as possible. This city exists in no single location. It is dispersed and distributed in much the same way as most global information networks, and yet it is inhabited by real people and things (not just data). To access this city one needs to buy into a very particular set of procedures and rules.

The airport brings to life a mutant geometry, a mobile polis of invasive security procedures and hyper-surveillance mixed in with the comfy banality of global franchising. It is a sublime 'non-place' that connects us to large-scale anonymous processes. With boarding pass in hand, we are on our way elsewhere, seemingly given unlimited access to any destination we can imagine. But, of course, this access is highly conditional. Though the walls and ramparts of this city are mostly virtual and shaped by the contours of information, our bodies are channelled in a manner that is not really determined by personal choice. As with much of the software packages we subscribe to today, we voluntarily lock into proprietary processes and infrastructures that are constantly being upgraded, updated and upended.

Aviopolis considers not only what airports mean, and how they are mediated to their users. We also consider what they do in terms of the materiality of the procedures that process both human and non-human commodity objects. This book is an exploration of the complex relations that exist between people and technology in global networked space.

In a world where mobility and connectivity of all kinds is increasing, the cultural significance of what we call the aviopolis has become apparent – for reasons ranging from security issues and civil rights, to urban planning and biometrics. Innovations in security (such as biometric processing), legislative exceptions (such as the USA's Homeland Security Bill) and transnational sovereignty (IATA and other global entities) are often tried out at the airport, before being introduced to the polis in general. If the contemporary airport has offered us 'laboratory conditions' to analyse the global interconnections of life in the information age, then perhaps it is an early-warning system for what might happen in the rest of the world under networked globalisation.

ANATOMY OF AN AIRPORT

AN AIRPORT PROCESSES TRAFFIC. IT IS A MACHINE FOR CAPTURING AND CONTROLLING FLOWS IN THE MOST LITERAL MANNER IMAGINABLE. THE MOVEMENTS OF PEOPLE, MACHINES AND CARGO, ARE PROGRAMMED TO KEEP A STEADY PACE AND FOLLOW DISTINCT TRAJECTORIES. OFTEN STAGED IN RELAYS FROM POINT TO POINT, EVERYTHING THAT MOVES AT AN AIRPORT MUST CONNECT TO A CERTAIN PART OF THE NETWORK AT A PARTICULAR MOMENT, AND THEN CONTINUE ITS JOURNEY ALONG PREDETERMINED PATHS AT A PRECISE VELOCITY.

ALL MOVEMENT IS CONTROLLED – FROM THE PLANES ON THE TARMAC TO THE CORRALLING OF PASSENGERS IN RETAIL AREAS. AS NODES IN A GLOBAL NETWORK OF MOVEMENT AIRPORT ARCHITECTURES FOLD THE LOCAL INTO THE GLOBAL, CONVERTING INFORMATION INTO TRAJECTORIES, AND CONSTRUCTING A TRANSITION FROM LANDSIDE TO AIRSIDE (AND VICE VERSA).

THESE MULTIPLE EXCHANGES BETWEEN DIFFERENT SYSTEMS CREATE A CONSTANT ELEMENT OF INSTABILITY. AIRPORTS, THEREFORE, DEPLOY MULTIPLE METHODS TO MAXIMALLY STABILISE ALL TRAVERSALS WITHIN THE SPHERE OF ITS CONTROL.

WHAT FOLLOWS IS A SNAPSHOT OF SOME OF THE LOGISTICAL, INSTITUTIONAL AND ARCHITECTURAL ELEMENTS THAT ENABLE AIRPORTS TO FACILITATE AND COMMODIFY MASS GLOBAL MOVEMENT.

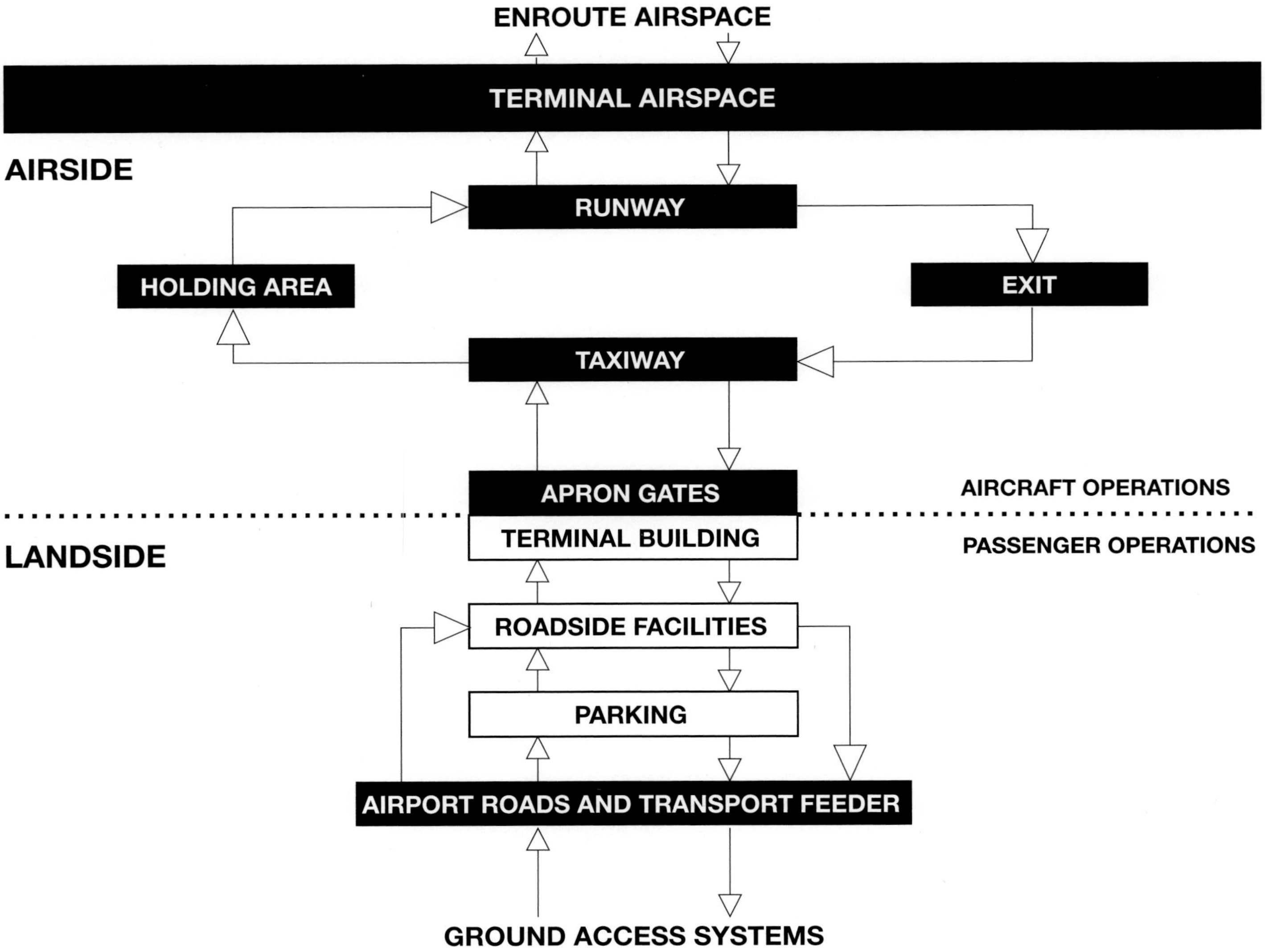

ENROUTE AIRSPACE

TERMINAL AIRSPACE

AIRSIDE

RUNWAY

HOLDING AREA

EXIT

TAXIWAY

APRON GATES

AIRCRAFT OPERATIONS

LANDSIDE

TERMINAL BUILDING

PASSENGER OPERATIONS

ROADSIDE FACILITIES

PARKING

AIRPORT ROADS AND TRANSPORT FEEDER

GROUND ACCESS SYSTEMS

The airport is a machine for processing things from land to air. All movement systems are designed around separation and flow, access and control. The airport is a complex machine, a series of interdependent and cross-referenced systems, functions, jurisdictions and modalities. What the airport is, depends on where you are in it, and how and why you are travelling through it. Internal processing is concerned with corporate or governmental screenings. Passengers and bags are cross-referenced, then sorted and packeted along different routes.

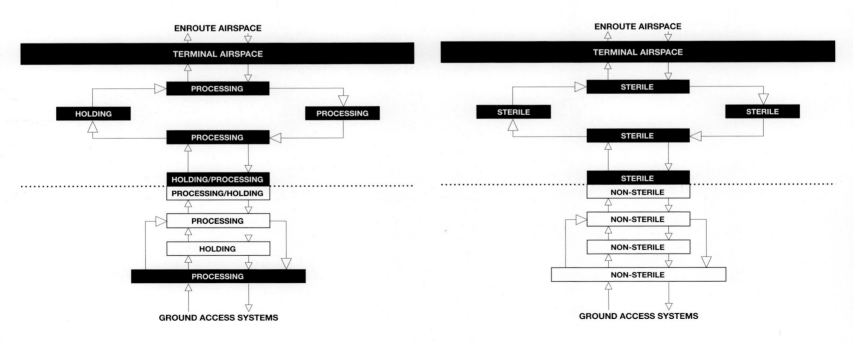

ENROUTE AIRSPACE

TERMINAL AIRSPACE

PROCESSING

HOLDING

PROCESSING

PROCESSING

HOLDING/PROCESSING
PROCESSING/HOLDING

PROCESSING

HOLDING

PROCESSING

GROUND ACCESS SYSTEMS

ENROUTE AIRSPACE

TERMINAL AIRSPACE

STERILE

STERILE

STERILE

STERILE

STERILE
NON-STERILE

NON-STERILE

NON-STERILE

NON-STERILE

GROUND ACCESS SYSTEMS

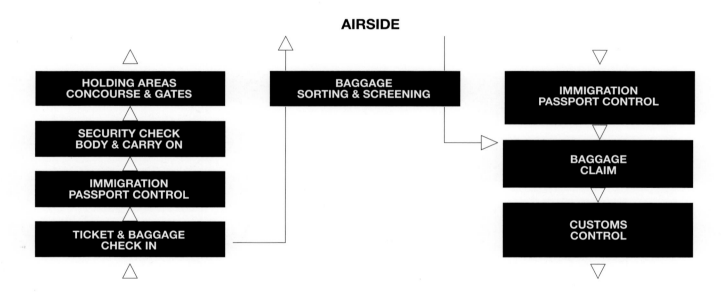

AIRSIDE

HOLDING AREAS
CONCOURSE & GATES

SECURITY CHECK
BODY & CARRY ON

IMMIGRATION
PASSPORT CONTROL

TICKET & BAGGAGE
CHECK IN

BAGGAGE
SORTING & SCREENING

IMMIGRATION
PASSPORT CONTROL

BAGGAGE
CLAIM

CUSTOMS
CONTROL

LANDSIDE

Projected volumes of curbside traffic

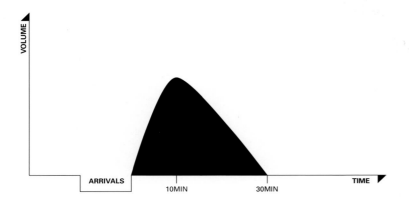

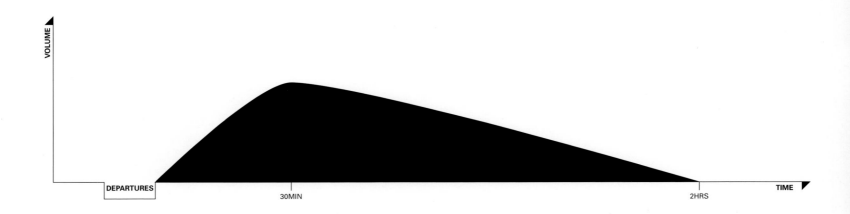

Most airports use elevated road systems to divide traffic into Arrivals and Departures.
Each of these uploading and downloading systems have distinct time frames.

Boeing 747 Turnaround Service

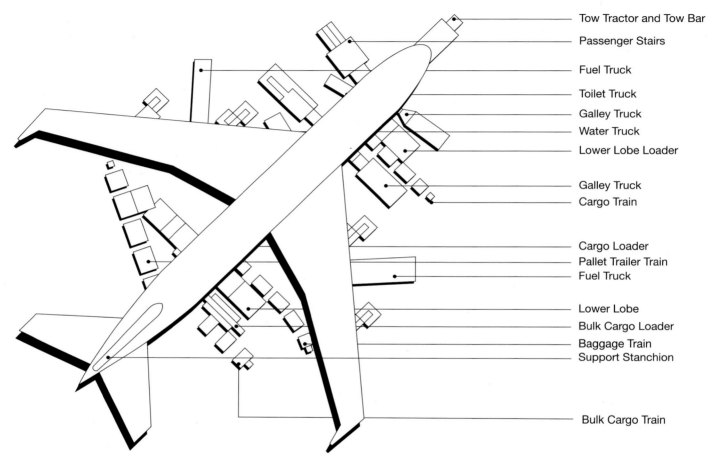

Tow Tractor and Tow Bar

Passenger Stairs

Fuel Truck

Toilet Truck

Galley Truck

Water Truck

Lower Lobe Loader

Galley Truck

Cargo Train

Cargo Loader

Pallet Trailer Train

Fuel Truck

Lower Lobe

Bulk Cargo Loader

Baggage Train

Support Stanchion

Bulk Cargo Train

Logistical precision governs all aspects of planning, design and operation at the airport. Each flow of movement is tabulated and tracked. Each component of the airport is designed to handle variable volumes of traffic.

It can take less than one hour to 'turnaround' a fully loaded long haul 747. Purpose built machinery plugs into a plane as soon as it arrives, downloading passengers, baggage, excretia, rubbish and uploading new passengers, new baggage, fuel, food and other necessities for life in the air.

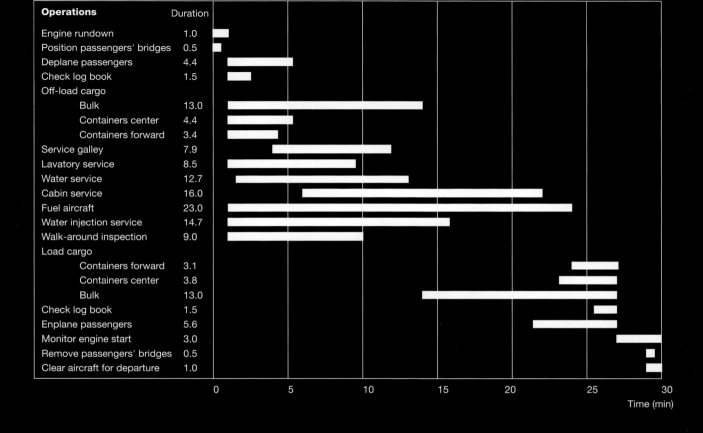

Operations	Duration
Engine rundown	1.0
Position passengers' bridges	0.5
Deplane passengers	4.4
Check log book	1.5
Off-load cargo	
Bulk	13.0
Containers center	4.4
Containers forward	3.4
Service galley	7.9
Lavatory service	8.5
Water service	12.7
Cabin service	16.0
Fuel aircraft	23.0
Water injection service	14.7
Walk-around inspection	9.0
Load cargo	
Containers forward	3.1
Containers center	3.8
Bulk	13.0
Check log book	1.5
Enplane passengers	5.6
Monitor engine start	3.0
Remove passengers' bridges	0.5
Clear aircraft for departure	1.0

Time (min)

This Gant chart indicates the processes, time frames and sequencing for servicing and turning around a 'typical jet' at the gate.
(Source Federal Aviation Authority.)

Tractor and pallet dolly.

Pushout tug and tow bar.

Transporter.

Mobile conveyor belt and pallet dollies.

Mobile generators (GPUs) provide power to planes while they are on the tarmac.

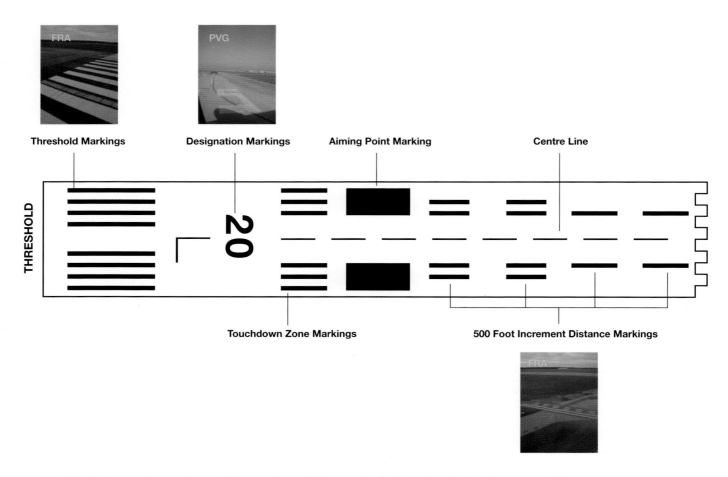

Threshold Markings

Designation Markings

Aiming Point Marking

Centre Line

THRESHOLD

20

Touchdown Zone Markings

500 Foot Increment Distance Markings

There is a sign for everything at the airport. Shape, colour and alphanumerics dominate the instructional language of the tarmac and terminal. All spaces of the airport are overlaid with signs.

Yellow centre lines guide planes from runway to gate.

Yellow lettering indicates location. These markers designate stop points for different jets.

White lines indicate thresholds between various airside zones.

Red lines indicate halt marks. You cannot cross this line without special authorisation.

SYD

B4 DOM2→

Yellow lettering with black background indicates a location.

Black lettering with a yellow background indicates destination. This sign indicates that we are on taxiway B4, and domestic terminal 2 is to the right.

Landside, airport signage separates various kinds of flow by creating a series of decision points that constantly split the potential routes for passengers until they arrive at their destination. Like all interface systems, alphanumeric and pictographic signage stabilises both system and user. You may not need to speak the language of the country to get around; but you do need to know the techno-cultural dialect of English – the international language of the airport.

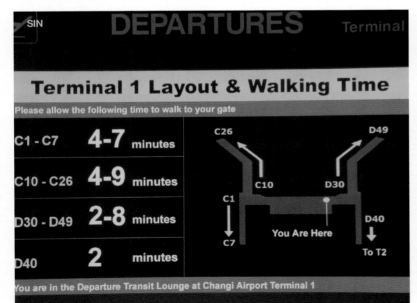

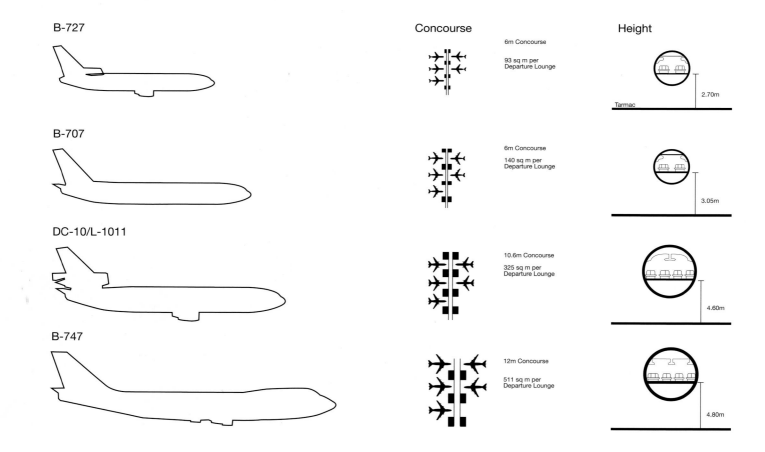

B-727

B-707

DC-10/L-1011

B-747

Concourse

6m Concourse

93 sq m per
Departure Lounge

6m Concourse

140 sq m per
Departure Lounge

10.6m Concourse

325 sq m per
Departure Lounge

12m Concourse

511 sq m per
Departure Lounge

Height

Tarmac

2.70m

3.05m

4.60m

4.80m

The form of airports is unstable, they are always upgrading. Since the introduction of jets, the general trend has been for planes to increase in size.

Airbus is currently developing the A380-800 series which will seat 555 passengers.

(after Blankenship)

TOTAL INTERNATIONAL AIRPORTS

SCHEDULED INTERNATIONAL IATA AIRPORTS 1,195
AIRPORTS UNDERGOING EXPANSION 225
NEW AIRPORTS OPENED 4
NEW AIRPORTS BEGUN 12

MOVEMENT: LIFE IN THE AIR CHANGES EVERYTHING ON THE GROUND

THE AIRPORT IS BUILT FOR TRANSIT. IT IS AN INTERCHANGE OF PEOPLE, MACHINES AND ITINERARIES. WHILE ALL AIRPORTS MAY NOT BE IDENTICAL, THERE IS A SAMENESS TO THEM THROUGHOUT THE WORLD. WHEREVER THE TRAVELLER IS IN THE WORLD, THEY KNOW WHERE THEY ARE WHEN THEY'RE AT THE AIRPORT. THEY'RE ON THEIR WAY TO SOMEWHERE ELSE. THE AIRPORT REPRESENTS 'LABORATORY CONDITIONS' FOR THINKING THROUGH THE TECHNO-CULTURAL PROCESSES AND SYSTEMS OF GLOBAL MOVEMENT.

IN THIS SECTION, WE CONSIDER THE OPERATIONS OF MOBILITY IN ORDER TO THINK ABOUT HOW NOTIONS OF 'CITIZEN' AND 'HUMAN' ARE BEING REDEFINED BY A NEW KIND OF TRANSIT-LIFE.

"IT'S ALL THIS AND MORE BESIDES."
FELIX GUATTARI

To the average Star Alliance member, the airport at Singapore, Los Angeles or Frankfurt would be as familiar as their local mall. As major hubs for global air traffic, many international passengers pass through one of these terminals almost every time they travel. Like a home-away-from-home, travellers can use the airport's business centre, smoke in the designated areas, take a nap in purpose built lounges, eavesdrop on conversations in themed environments, or buy American cigarettes at a good price. Steeped in habits learned from a lifetime of roads and shopping malls, the denizens of aviopolis move from terminal to terminal, from gate to gate with a methodical certainty. Many of these frequent flyers have, of course, never really been to Singapore, LA or Frankfurt. They never leave the airport. Singapore, for instance – whatever that entity may be – remains abstract, a concept gleaned through newspaper reports, stories told by friends and colleagues, and by time spent at its airport. They may never have been 'to Singapore', but they have been 'in Singapore'. On their way elsewhere, the occupants of aviopolis press against the nation's frontiers from somewhere within its geophysical borders. At the airport, the idea of border loses its physical dimensions and reconfigures as a series of protocols and passwords that can appear anywhere.

Speed shrinks space, traversing borders that once seemed so stable. Telephone lines, radio waves and jet travel have all changed the geography of the world, replacing relations of distance and space with what seminal technology theorist Paul Virilio calls "chronography", which measures distance in terms of time and speed.[1] At the airport the most obvious signifier for this is revealed in the answer to the question "How long was your flight?" The answer is generally given in hours not miles. Distance is a temporal rather than a spatial issue. How long is a flight? How long does something take to download? Such questions are indicative of a peculiarly networked logic, where issues like 'access' and 'flow' dominate a new set of international rules and protocols that cut through the geo-physical borders of the nation states in which we live. This process, whereby power rewrites the rules of space by creating new thresholds and new borders, may be intense at present, but the process itself isn't new. Colonialism reorganised geographical space into sovereign zones of ideological and economic allegiances. Place became *terra nullius* long ago, wiped of indigenous particularities and incorporated into a totalising space of urgent global improvement. But as Virilio also notes, speed propels geo-politics into other dimensions.

At the crossroads of this transition is the airport, where the chrono-politics of jet travel collide with the remnants of national geo-politics. In other words, airports enact another way of thinking about global relationships. They quite literally operate through a 'network logic' that cuts across the categories of nation states and territory, humans and animals, products and machines, and material and informational modes of mobility and reconnects them in new relationships to each other.

In the early 1990s, design critic Deyan Sudjic noted that airports were "high-stress landscapes, full of anxious people on unfamiliar territory".[2] But things are always upgrading and therefore changing

World's 30 Busiest Airports
As at October 2003 – Total Passengers Enplaned and Deplaned

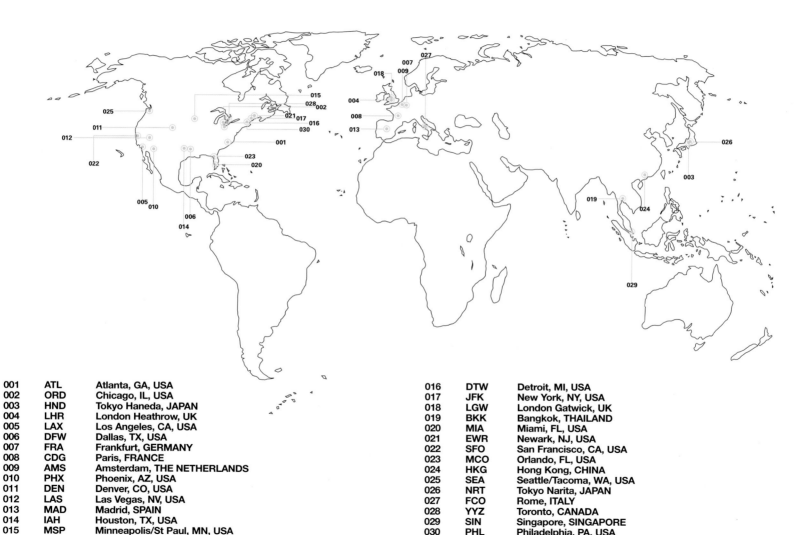

001	ATL	Atlanta, GA, USA
002	ORD	Chicago, IL, USA
003	HND	Tokyo Haneda, JAPAN
004	LHR	London Heathrow, UK
005	LAX	Los Angeles, CA, USA
006	DFW	Dallas, TX, USA
007	FRA	Frankfurt, GERMANY
008	CDG	Paris, FRANCE
009	AMS	Amsterdam, THE NETHERLANDS
010	PHX	Phoenix, AZ, USA
011	DEN	Denver, CO, USA
012	LAS	Las Vegas, NV, USA
013	MAD	Madrid, SPAIN
014	IAH	Houston, TX, USA
015	MSP	Minneapolis/St Paul, MN, USA

016	DTW	Detroit, MI, USA
017	JFK	New York, NY, USA
018	LGW	London Gatwick, UK
019	BKK	Bangkok, THAILAND
020	MIA	Miami, FL, USA
021	EWR	Newark, NJ, USA
022	SFO	San Francisco, CA, USA
023	MCO	Orlando, FL, USA
024	HKG	Hong Kong, CHINA
025	SEA	Seattle/Tacoma, WA, USA
026	NRT	Tokyo Narita, JAPAN
027	FCO	Rome, ITALY
028	YYZ	Toronto, CANADA
029	SIN	Singapore, SINGAPORE
030	PHL	Philadelphia, PA, USA

at the airport. Before September 11, most air travellers had become used to the hybrid structures of an ever-evolving airspace system, slumping into the banality of the frustrating routines of travelling. The airport interface was no longer exotic, but had become as familiar as any global franchise – part mall, part theme park, part check point. Now, three years after these "terrible events", security offers a different spectacle where anxiety is integrated into the logic of queues (which themselves play upon the frustrating feelings of powerlessness and entrapment, of not being able to move). And yet all of this does not mean that airports no longer hold an allure. The airport is still the site of take-off, a dramatic ascent into the vertical realm, with all its attendant tropes of power and transcendence. The modern airport still offers that *frisson* of danger that characterised the very early years of aviation – "a reversal of gravity, a death defied", as writer Donald Pascoe has recently put it.[3]

Arrivals

Strictly speaking, there is no 'first airport'. Records indicate that operational airports existed as far back as 1909. Most of these early aerodromes were rudimentary, often a convenient repurposing of local athletic fields, parks and golf courses. Some of these airstrips were upgraded into regional airports and private landing fields. Others expanded into the terminal cities of Sydney, Newark and Orly, while a few morphed back into fields and farmlands. Sydney Airport, for instance, has been in continuous operation since 1920, developing from a modest airstrip in the middle of a swamp-lined paddock on the northern shore of Botany Bay. For 80 years this airport has been 'terraforming' its environs, sucking highways and rail corridors towards it, re-zoning its surrounding suburbs, flattening houses and changing the geography of the city around it.

Although the story of each airport is intimately connected to a most unique sense of place – Botany Bay in Sydney or Idlewild Field in New York – the spatial history of airports, whether New York or

Sydney, follows a repetitive trajectory: a marshland on the outskirts of town becomes a landing strip, which is later paved. Old sheds become international airports. Part of the history of airports concerns the ceaseless remediation of the awkward materialities of place (like swamps and farming lands) into space that can be measured, represented and standardised.

Forever upgrading into something new and better, the airport is never complete. It is in a constant state of adaptation with the techno-cultural processes that constitute its operations. When jet travel went commercial in the late 1950s, many terminals became obsolete (the most famous being Eero Saarinen's futuristic TWA terminal at New York International, later renamed John F Kennedy International). Airports had to be re-engineered to accommodate bigger planes and the higher throughput of passengers associated with the upgrading of technology (e.g. the introduction of faster and bigger jet planes). Speed overtook the airport itself.

The history of airports provides a telling snapshot of how techno-cultural innovations (such as cars or planes) and economic-political contingencies (like wars and the rise of liberal capitalism) can quite literally rewire cultural landscapes. The airport is an immanent system constantly overcoming its own limitations, branching into new dimensions and making new connections. Airstrips became airports, and airports became movies; points of memory and points of departure, sites of industry, military zones, shopping malls, brand names and more. The airport has evolved into a complex techno-cultural machine. It provides an interface not simply between material components (e.g. structures for processing from land to air). The airport's interface functions at a variety of levels, both material and immaterial, global and local. Airports stabilise contexts across distinct systems enabling a multitude of things to access its nodes. Planes, people, cars, aviation fuel, freight, and catering are constantly plugging in, peeling off or just passing through the airport. Airports are multi-platform, multi-dimensional, multi-tasking movement machines.

Like a complex overlapping of co-evolving biotechnical systems, airports around the world process millions of things (people, messages, cargo, missions, procedures) in unlimited combinations every day. Yet out of this incredible movement of multiple textures a remarkable sameness in structure seems to contain this virtual diversity. For all the speed and radical heterogeneity of global air travel, a refrain of aviation aesthetics has emerged in the contemporary architecture of airports – the beep of metal detection, the expanses of glass overlooking the apron, the international pictograms, the slick retail space. This refrain seems to soothe the disorientation produced by the constancy of transit in modern lives, where the imperatives of advance and upgrade are pre-emptive in every way: new home renovations, new technologies, new democracies, new faces. And yet despite the 'newness', everything seems to be converging into sameness. Every renovation has a water feature, every face has Nicole Kidman's nose, every democracy is becoming an American franchise and every airport speaks English. In this life of constant upgrade and movement we are assured that the future will somehow be rosier and more certain if we yield to flow and move with the rest of the traffic.

The integrated flows of aviation were not always so seamless. Flying was once the adventure of the reckless and the dashing. Unreliable aircraft generated real anxieties for a potential public up until the 1960s. Flying was uncomfortable, noisy, turbulent and expensive. Small propeller planes flew at low bumpy altitudes, stopping frequently to refuel. In the early 1960s, 70 per cent of the most frequent flying nation in the world, the USA, had never taken a commercial flight.[4]

Modern jet aviation reassured passengers' underlying anxiety about air travel. As traffic increased so did the complexity of corporate, individualist and nationalist forces that regulated airports into nodes of a symbolic, moral and material economy of global movement. Much of this regulation occurs through the airport's diagrammatics of technical compliance: a runway must be so long and so wide, and a departure gate must be able to accommodate a series of different

model planes. The variety of internationalist protocols, immigration, flight path routing, safety standards, corporate 'customer focus', airside management, signage systems, landside access and flow management converge and create architectures of global logistics. While all airports may not be identical, there is a sameness to them throughout the world. Wherever you are in the world, you know where you are when you're at the airport. You are on your way somewhere else.

Transit

According to French anthropologist Marc Augé, today we live in a world,

> … where people are born in the clinic and die in the hospital, where transit points and temporary abodes are proliferating under luxurious or inhuman conditions (hotel chains and squats, holiday camps and refugee camps, shantytowns threatened with demolition or doomed to festering longevity); where a dense network of means of transport which are also inhabited spaces are developing; where the *habitué* of supermarkets, slot machines and credit cards communicate wordlessly, through gestures, with an abstract, unmediated commerce: a world thus surrendered to solitary individuality, to the fleeting, the temporary and ephemeral.[5]

This is a world of constant transit. At any given moment, about three million people spend at least part of their day being propelled in superlight alloy cocoons across the sky. However, the world of transit doesn't operate at the same velocity, or in the same modes in every place. For instance, the USA is, by far, the number one nation in terms of total-tonne-kilometres and passenger-kilometres. Of the over 1.6 billion passengers moved in global civilian airspace in 2003, 36 per cent were carried on US-badged airlines. Of the top 25 airports in the world in terms of passenger throughput, 17 are located in the USA. The world's busiest airport, Atlanta's Hartsfield, processes around 78 million passengers per year. Chicago's

O'Hare, the world's second busiest airport, processes 72.5 million passengers per year. Both of these airports are major domestic hub airports and US traffic is overwhelmingly commuter-based and domestic.[6]

As a machine for processing and controlling mobility, the airport operates according to the seemingly paradoxical logic of transit, where 'stop systems' (like border control, baggage and identity checks) integrate with 'go systems' (like capacity and flow control techniques). The two essential documents for moving, the passport and the boarding pass, represent the different logics of stop and go and respect two distinct but related sovereignties. One authenticates national citizenship by verifying identity while the other scans the co-ordinates of logistical units into the global and corporate network of aviation.

Like data in a network, packets of information-made-flesh are transmitted to other places. For instance, as the citizen of aviopolis travels from Sydney to Egypt, they engage in a series of mostly involuntary protocols. They are routed through the geography of IATA acronyms in set ways: SYD/SIN/CAI (Sydney-Singapore-Cairo). If that is unavailable they could reroute SYD/BKK/CAI (Sydney-Bangkok-Cairo).

Cairo Airport may look nothing like Singapore's Changi Airport, but its information architecture is the same – it is designed to process mobility. It is a self-renewing machine that 'refreshes' after each take-off and landing. Planes download passengers, baggage, cargo, excreta, and rubbish, and, then, upload passengers, baggage, cargo, fuel, food and packaged gadgets. The airport propels and regulates direction and flow. The sky is turned into bandwidth as planes move along specified air corridors.

Each piece of baggage is scanned and tracked and matched with regulated precision. There is a path and position for everything at the airport. Media theorist, Scott Bukatman notes that although the airport may be like a mall, "the airport doesn't deny the outside

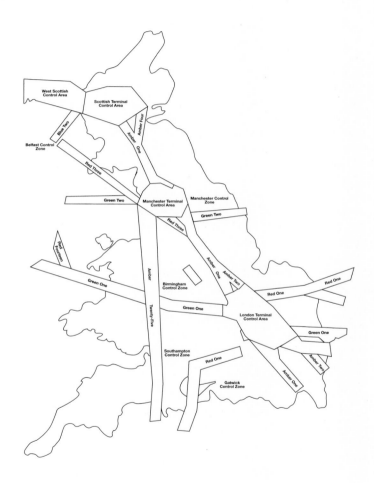

All airspace is tightly controlled. This diagram shows the major highways of the air over England.

world – it just privileges directionality".[7] A destination firmly in mind, we 'wayfind' through the airport, negotiating the banal procedures of check in, immigration and security with the exotic (in every sense of the word) promises of an 'other' space. At the airport the near and the elsewhere coalesce into a series of macro- and micro-connected itineraries that are simultaneously real and mythical.

The airport not only transforms a body on the ground into a body in the air, but it also involves the incorporeal transformation of the travelling body into a series of processing categories, like citizen, passenger, baggage allowance, threat (code red) or innocent. The airport constitutes a space where a series of contractual declarations (I am Australian, I have nothing to declare, I packed these bags myself) accumulate into a password where one is free to deterritorialise on a literal level – one may take flight, but not without a cost. Scanned, checked and made to feel guilty – one could be a smuggler, a terrorist, an illegal alien, a disease vector. The categories of 'guilt' expand constantly.

Orientation

In the pursuit of our itinerary, the place – that ethnographic imaginary of organic sociality – becomes little more than a sign saying 'you are here'. In our need to move, we submit to a series of invasive procedures and security checks that are becoming pervasive and yet are still rationalised through a discourse of exception – "Only at the airport". In transit spaces one doesn't see landscape as one sees landmarks (and oneself) indefinitely 'othered' as pax, citizen, consumer, security risk, traveller or anonymous free spirit. As the passenger moves through the airport, they focus on symbols for orientation and pass through thresholds that authenticate identity. As Marc Augé says "there will be no individualisation (no right to anonymity) without identity checks".[8]

At the airport place is turned into passage and identity is transformed into a biometric (literally, the measure of life). The airport is a non-place: its *topos* is primarily symbolic and transitory; its sociality is solitary and contractual.

Non-places are increasing – everywhere we are addressed as agents of one kind or another in a landscape of signs – "do not eat on the train", "shop at 'HeathLow'", "please present boarding pass and passport" – yet this agency is highly modulated. The conditions of traffic or the rules of use address a virtual 'average man' subject to a series of silent exchanges and injunctions (turn left, insert card now, Welcome to Chicago), where contractual modes of interaction are sharply defined and textually mediated. Yet if the non–places of supermodernity are so overwhelmingly contractual and solitary, why can driving down the highway or walking to the departure gate feel so liberating?

In Michel Serres' ficto-critical exploration of the networked world of airports, *Angels*, one of his frequent flying characters, Pantope, eulogises on the joys of jet travel:

> The wild passion of letting yourself be transported by wind, by burning heat and by cold space… the pleasure of being anonymous, of being quiet for a long time, of existing in no place at all… where the dialogues of others continually slip in… the pleasure of leaving, of being far away, of being missing… the subtle pleasures of erasing the presence of your body, your words and your shadow, of counting for nothing, of hiding yourself, of becoming so light that you fly away….[9]

There is something pleasurable about the motionless motion and placeless place of jet aviation. There is a certain sublimeness in becoming airborne, anonymous, absent, and a corresponding banality to becoming stuck and identified. In the world of transit, operational logic is utterly calibrated to movement. Everything is organised around motion. By dint of this ontological twist from 'being' to 'becoming' (as a material organisational principle) a whole series of previously held concepts organised around more static concepts like category or position don't seem to have the

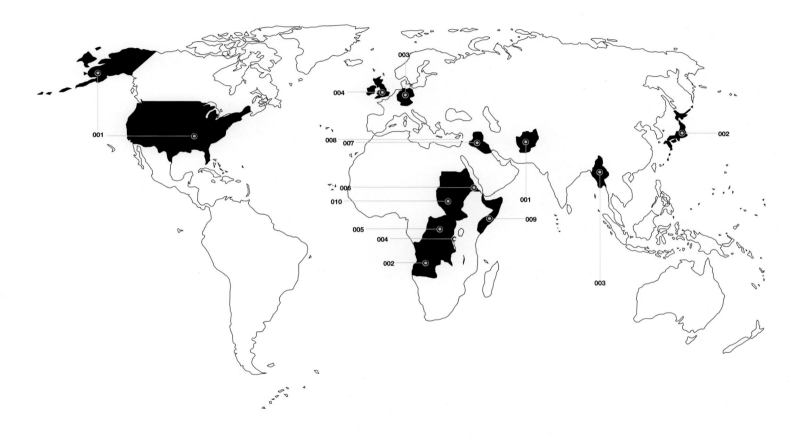

Top Four Nations For Total Volume Of Traffic
(Passengers, Freight, Mail) Year Ending 2002

001	USA	31 per cent
002	Japan	6 per cent
003	Germany	5 per cent
004	United Kingdom	5 per cent

Top Ten Source Countries For Refugees
78 Per Cent Of All Refugess Come From Ten Countries. Year Ending 2002

001	Afghanistan		006	Eritrea
002	Angola		007	Iraq
003	Burma		008	Palestine
004	Burundi		009	Somalia
005	Congo-Kinshasa		010	Sudan

same purchase on the real as they once did. In the case of airports, operations are set toward the dynamic unities of traffic, rather than the categories and positions of particular planes. The world is on the move. Money, people, machines, data whirl around the planet, and in so doing the world necessarily changes: new continuities and discontinuities emerge. There is a time-space recalibration that is at one level totalising (producing standardised networks of material and information highways, generic travel experiences and 'by the numbers' biometric processing), but which at another level is deeply personal: the discontinuities of mass-migration, mass-transit and mass-media produce actual lives and 'real' experiences.

When citizenship of a mass-transit world entails neither blood (born of citizen parents) nor soil (born in sovereign territory), as in many 'multicultural' countries, like the USA or Britain, "the continuity of man and citizen, nativity and nationality" is broken – and with it some of the fundamental presuppositions of modern sovereignty.[10] Travellers, immigrants and refugees may be 'released' from the shackles of earthly citizenship, out of which new virtual relationships emerge. But on the whole, at the airport, these relationships are coagulated into highly public and semioticised contractualities. As theorists of biopower, such as Giorgio Agamben, and theorists of globalisation, like Manuel Castells, have noted, states don't deal well with the strange particularities of networked and virtualised individuals.[11] They prefer to keep the subject within more knowable constraints of identity.

Departures

"The tradition of the oppressed teaches us that the 'state of emergency' in which we live is not the exception but the rule."
Walter Benjamin[12]

At the airport the upside of transformational possibilities, of being given the 'all clear' to become a passenger, or a businessman or a traveller, is only available to the 'innocent'. And the technical nature

of innocence is changing. The airport is in a constant state of emergency – its structures prepare constantly for disaster. As shoes are searched and fire teams do drills, innocence is not presumed: it must be proven. After September 11, examples of the exception becoming the rule are myriad. Any skin irritation is a possible case of anthrax, rather than a more common allergy. Every Muslim is a possible terrorist.

The markers of identity which may once have derived from the cross-matching of body to passport have expanded into more comprehensive modes of biometrics in which iris scans and face recognition systems, nationality, bank accounts, age/gender/ethnic profiles and itineraries assemble innocence – which also becomes the criteria of an increasingly complex virtual identity. (No wonder we want to get inside the plane to feel the embrace of anonymity.) For Giorgio Agamben, every attempt to rethink the political space of the West must begin with a clear awareness that we no longer know anything of the classical distinction between private life and political existence, between man as biological life and between man's political existence in the city. All forms of life have merged into a form of what he calls 'bare life', where the social and biological body opens up directly to political power.

For Agamben, bare life is the state of pervasive exception where "power confronts nothing but pure life, without any mediation". Agamben focuses on the more extreme bio-politics of the west, which manifested in Nazi policies of genocide and human experimentation. Yet unlike much of the voluminous contemporary Holocaust literature in which the procedural and systemic operations of power are exceptionalised into a humanist narrative of atrocity and thus comfortably resolved with "never again", Agamben claims that the so called 'exception' of the Holocaust lays the ground rules for life today. It has been over 70 years since Walter Benjamin took flight from Germany, and yet unsurprisingly his damning insights on the rhetorical functions of 'progress' and 'the future' – "the current amazement that the things we are experiencing are 'still' possible in the twentieth century is *not* philosophical" – are especially

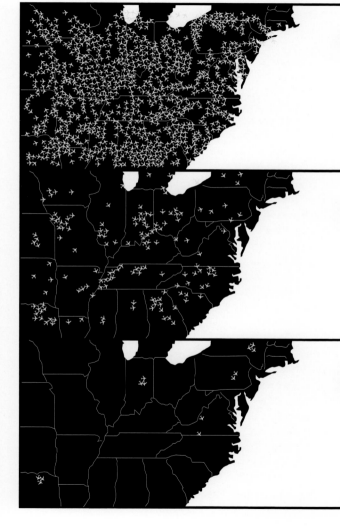

SEPTEMBER 11 2001
09:49 AM
3,667 FLIGHTS

SEPTEMBER 11 2001
10:35 AM
1,147 FLIGHTS

SEPTEMBER 11 2001
11:40 AM
290 FLIGHTS

prescient as the 'war on terror' legislates exceptional provisions to bypass the global rules of war, as well as the national constitutions of many liberal democracies.[13]

Transit Life

If freedom of movement is one of the most elemental of freedoms, then the camp provides the ultimate backdrop to the sublime feelings of placelessness that many experience as they wander through the airport. The camp, like the airport, is built for transit. Yet in the camp, no one moves. Both airport and camp constitute zones of exception. Each is framed by a rhetoric of emergency, each limits concepts of the other. One facilitates movement and the other denies it, yet both are zones of perpetual transit and futuristic promise.

The asylum seeker held in Australia's infamous Baxter detention centre is there on a promise that protection and a life elsewhere is at hand. As they wait, for sometimes up to three years, over 60 million passengers have transited through the terminals at Sydney. On the other side of the world, Israeli bulldozers destroy Palestinian houses and farms to complete a 400 kilometres network of 'settler by-pass roads' which are off-limits to Palestinians, ostensibly for security reasons. These roads criss-cross the West Bank and connect illegal Israeli settlements to each other and Israel's 1948 borders. The effects of these roads are twofold: they materially hook Palestinian land into the Israeli road traffic network, further fragmenting the territory of Palestine; and they duplicate the most modern of time/space displacements in a land overburdened with history: this is the production of a non-place. The Holy Land becomes a type of Hollywood. Like the commuters of LA who can drive for years and never see the slums below, Israelis can travel through Palestine along the settler roads and never encounter an Arab.

All spaces today are complex and multi-dimensional. As cultural theorist Michel Foucault puts it,

We are in the epoch of simultaneity: we are in the epoch of juxtaposition, the epoch of the near and the far, of the side by side, of the dispersed. We are at the moment, I believe, when our experience of the world is less that of a long life developing through time than that of a network that connects points and intersects with its own skein.[14]

Increasingly, life is a series of itineraries and transit stops: home to work, gym to supermarket, Sydney to London, the Middle East to a detention centre (and increasingly, deportation back). Transit life is the life form of this millennium. If the nation state is floundering, control moves from geophysical borders to borders of jurisdiction which themselves are constantly upgrading in response to 'new threats'. The polis itself is increasingly organised through the logic of exception and flow control that dominates the airport. As Deyan Sudjic notes, "the transience of the airport embodies contemporary urbanism in a real, as well as a metaphorical sense".[15] As the centre of our home city, Sydney, undergoes another upgrade and new motorways cut into the ground so that we can travel from the centre to satellite surburbs miles away and never see a single suburban street or house, we know Sudjic and Virilio are right: the airport is the city of the future. But what of Agamben's claim that "the camp, which is now securely lodged within the city's interior, is the new biopolitical *nomos* of the planet"?[16]

For Agamben, any zone where normal order is suspended is a camp. A camp is a space where anything is possible (including death). New camps emerge daily: dogs sniff commuters on trains, detention centres are a growth industry and the category of refugee is constantly being redefined. The post war refugee, the brave dissident fleeing communist regimes, has been upgraded to become the queue jumper and the illegal alien. Over at the airport, in the interests of efficiency, the traveller too has undergone some upgrading. The sophisticated experience of the jetset traveller of the 1960s is now available only to those travellers in business class or with the right loyalty scheme. The rest are now in the queue, as well, waiting for a bag search and body pat down.

1   Virilio, Paul and Lotringer, Sylvere, *Pure War,* New York: semiotext(e), 1983.

2   Sudjic, Deyan, *The 100 Mile City,* London: Flamingo, 1992, p. 169.

3   Pascoe, Donald, *Airspaces,* London: Reaktion Books, 2001, p. 45.

4   Cited in Lewis, William, *Airlines Executives and Federal Regulation; case studies in American enterprise from the airmail era to the dawn of the jet age,* Columbus: Ohio State University Press, 2000, p. 34.

5   Augé, Marc, *Non-places: An Introduction to an Anthropology of Supermodernity*, J Howe trans, London: Verso, 1995, p. 78.

6   All figures from ICOA Annual Report 2002.

7   Bukatman, Scott, *Terminal Identity: The Virtual Subject in Postmodern Science Fiction*, Durham: Duke University Press, 1993, p. 126.

8   Augé, *Non-places,* p. 102.

9   Serres, Michel, *Angels: a Modern Myth,* Paris: Flammarion, 1995, p. 262.

10 Agamben, Giorgio, *Means without End,* V Binetti & C. Casarino trans, Minneapolis: University of Minnesota Press, 2000, p. 131.

11 Castells, Manuel, *The Rise of the Network Society,* Vol. 1, Oxford: Blackwell, 1998.

12 Benjamin, Walter, "Theses on the Philosophy of History" in *Illuminations*, Hannah Arendt trans, London: Fontana, 1992, p. 248.

13 Benjamin, Illuminations, p. 249.

14 Foucault, Michel, "Of Other Spaces", *Diacritics*, Vol. 16, No. 1, 1986, p. 22.

15 Sudjic, *The 100 Mile City,* p. 152.

16 Agamben, Giorgio, *Homo Sacer: Sovereign Power and Bare Life,* Daniel Heller-Roazen trans, Stanford: Stanford University Press, 1998, p. 176.

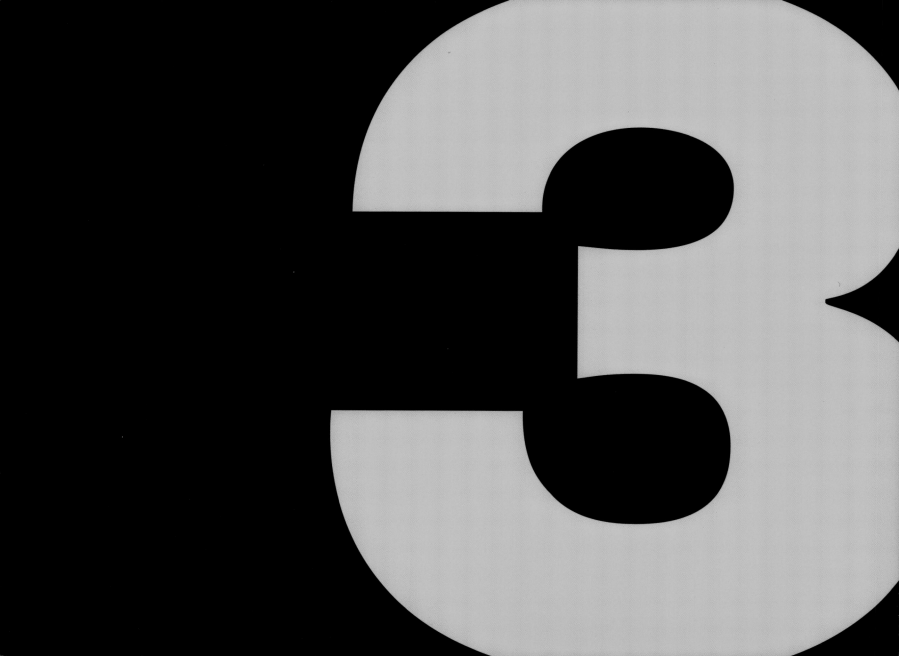

FROM THE JET AGE TO THE NETWORK MALL

THE MODERN AIRPORT EVOLVED OUT OF THE CONVERGING
OPERATIONS OF COMMERCIAL, GOVERNMENTAL, MILITARY
AND PRIVATE INTERESTS. IN THE USA, CIVIL AVIATION
BEGAN WITH A GOVERNMENT RUN AIRMAIL SERVICE,
WHICH ACCOUNTED FOR THE VAST MAJORITY OF CIVIL
AVIATION UNTIL 1925. AS AIRMAIL TRAFFIC INCREASED,
FEDERAL AUTHORITIES BEGAN TO DIVEST THEMSELVES OF
THE COSTLY ACTIVITY OF AVIATION AND ITS ASSOCIATED
INFRASTRUCTURE AND BEGAN TO ENCOURAGE PRIVATE
INTERESTS. THE KELLY ACT OF 1925 AWARDED ALL THE
MAIL SERVICES ASSOCIATED WITH THE PROFITABLE NEW
YORK-CHICAGO-SAN FRANCISCO ROUTE TO PRIVATE
CONTRACTORS. PASSENGER SERVICES WERE INITIALLY
DEPENDENT ON GOVERNMENT POLICIES THAT LINKED
PROFITABLE MAIL CONTRACTS TO THE LESS PROFITABLE
CARGO OF HUMAN PASSENGERS.

Passenger services have always been one of the least stable sectors of aviation and remain secondary to military aviation in terms of profitability, as well as research and development. Civil aviation, like telecommunications, has had vigorous competition on profitable main routes, and airlines have had national obligations to service less-profitable regional routes. The introduction of jet aircraft, such as the Boeing 707 (itself a spin-off of military aviation research), provided a major boost to the flagging civil aviation industry. Faster, quieter, more comfortable and able to fly longer without refuelling, jets began to make passenger services financially viable. The first full jet services in the early 1960s spawned a new popular vision of aviation as accessible to the 'common man' – flight itself had become a commodity.

Jet Age airports staged this popular vision by way of their architecture, entwining capitalism and glamour in order to invoke a particularly optimistic vision of the future. Their individualistic shapes and vaulting interiors helped to sell and promote the idea that anyone could access the limitless horizons that had previously been the provenance of the rich and powerful. The age of the Jet Set popularised the practice of global travel and put it up for sale as a piece of the future, as part of progress.

Unfortunately, however, the future quickly turned out to look less like a *Thunderbirds* set and began to resemble something more like a building site. None of the great Jet Age airports – like Eero Saarinen's terminals at John F Kennedy and Dulles Airports – have remained 'intact'. The very notion of modernist progress that gave rise to these structures also guaranteed their demise. None of these airports could remain unchanged in the face of the constant technological improvements the aviation industry delivered. Almost as soon as these terminals were completed, new longer wide-bodied jets made them virtually obsolete. The only way to save these edifices was to subject them to a long tiresome series of renovations, none of which ever seemed adequate to the needs of the present.

Today, those Jet Age terminals that remain are usually buried within the shells of supersized airports that have grown around them. While the original Jet Age terminals are generally associated with the post war boom in the United States, a new Jet Age is underway in China, where the ninth Five Year Plan sets out the building and development of 41 airports.

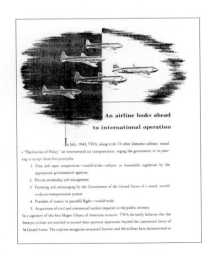

"The Airline and Your Community", a 78 page promotional booklet produced by TWA in 1943.

"HISTORY RECORDS THE STORIES OF MANY CITIES THAT HAVE ACHIEVED WORLD IMPORTANCE BY REASON OF NATURAL OR STRATEGIC ADVANTAGES, ONLY TO FADE INTO OBSCURITY BECAUSE OF THEIR FAILURE OR INABILITY TO ADAPT THEMSELVES TO DEVELOPMENTS IN TRANSPORTATION AND COMMUNICATION."* THESE INTRODUCTORY REMARKS WERE QUOTED BY THE PLANNERS OF NEW YORK-NEW JERSEY AIRPORTS SYSTEM AS PART OF DOCUMENT ARGUING FOR A THIRD MAJOR AIRPORT AT IDLEWILD FIELD. NEW YORK INTERNATIONAL AIRPORT WAS RENAMED JOHN F KENNEDY INTERNATIONAL IN 1963.

Elevation sketch of the International Arrival Building at New York's Terminal City, originally appeared in "New York International Airport: aerial gateway to the United States", 15 page brochure produced by the Port Authority of New York, 1957. *Regional Planning Association, New York, 1947

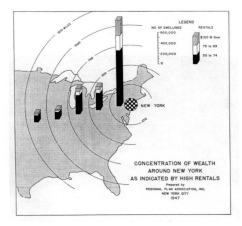

Demographic chart reproduced in "Airports of Tomorrow: a report of the regional airport conference on its plan for development of an airport system for the New York metropolitan region", a publication of the Regional Plan Association, New York, 1947.

Artist's conception of the future terminal city at New York International, Idlewild. PANYNY Planning Documents, 2001

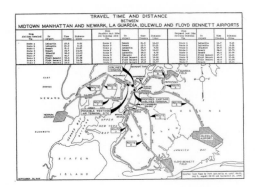

Travel, time and distance chart reproduced in "Airports of Tomorrow".

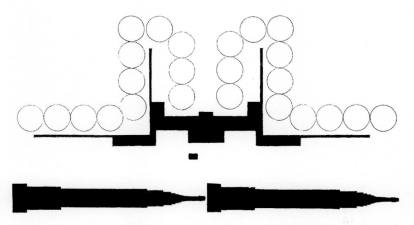

International Arrival Building and Airline Wings, the main building group at New York International Airport's Terminal Area, was almost as long as two Empire State Buildings (381 metres high) laid on their sides end to end. Originally published in The Port of New York Authority press release, Monday 21 February 1955.

Idlewild as it was, 1939.

Proposed development for Idlewild, 1949.

Idlewild seen from the air, 1942.

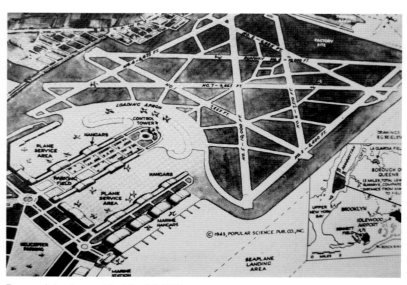

Proposed development for Idlewild, 1943.

Aviopolis A Book About Airports

Artist's conception of the main entrance to the International Arrival Building, showing the elevated promenade and control tower. The Airline Wing Building East and two individual airline terminal buildings are visible in the background. Originally published in The Port of New York Authority press release, Monday 21 February 1955.

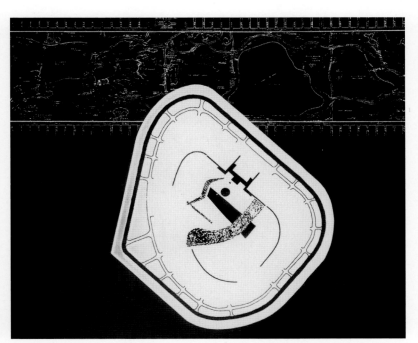

Passenger Terminal Area constructed at New York International Airport was projected to cover 265 hectares, more than three-quarters the size of Central Park (339 hectares). Terminal City and Central Park are shown here in the same scale. Originally published in The Port of New York Authority press release, Monday 21 February 1955.

Artist's conception of the Passenger Terminal Area, New York International Airport, originally published in The Port of New York Authority press release, Monday 21 February 1955.

New York International Airport, 1962, featuring the original terminals.

JFK from the air, 1971.

Aerial view of JFK featuring the control tower, 1990.

Previous page: JFK from the air, 2001.

Idlewild, at the beginning, showing the original Terminal City master plan, 1958.

Plan for the restoration and construction of the TWA terminal redevelopment. From "JFK Sites 5/6 Redevelopment Including the TWA Terminal" planning document, Port Authority of New York and New Jersey, 2001.

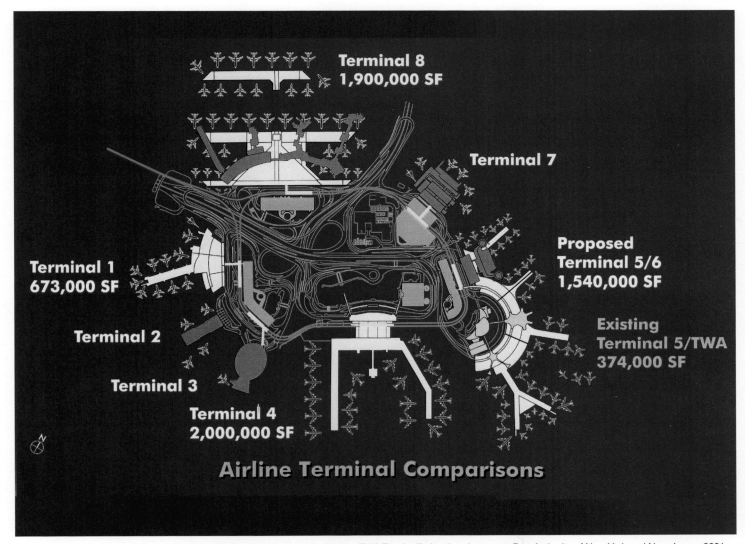

Terminal 8
1,900,000 SF

Terminal 7

Proposed
Terminal 5/6
1,540,000 SF

Terminal 1
673,000 SF

Existing
Terminal 5/TWA
374,000 SF

Terminal 2

Terminal 3

Terminal 4
2,000,000 SF

Airline Terminal Comparisons

Airline terminal comparisons, from "JFK Sites 5/6 Redevelopment Including the TWA Terminal" planning document, Port Authority of New York and New Jersey, 2001.

Left: Proposed changes to landside, terminal, and airside congfigurations around the historic TWA terminal. From "JFK Sites 5/6 Redevelopment Including the TWA Terminal" planning document, Port Authority of New York and New Jersey, 2001.

Right: Comparison of old and proposed new terminal configurations of the TWA terminal. From "JFK Sites 5/6 Redevelopment Including the TWA Terminal" planning document, Port Authority of New York and New Jersey, 2001.

THE TWA TERMINAL AT JFK, A GLORIOUSLY ROMANTIC MONUMENT TO BRAND DEVELOPMENT, CEASED OPERATING IN 2002 AND HAS BECOME AN HISTORIC RUIN. THE TERMINAL OPENED IN 1961, JUST AS HIGHER CAPACITY JETS, LIKE THE BOEING 707, CAME INTO REGULAR SERVICE AND CREATED MORE CAPACITY AND TURNOVER THAN THE AIRPORT COULD COPE WITH (BOTH AIRSIDE AND LANDSIDE). THE TERMINAL IS UNDER REDEVELOPMENT TO BETTER EXPLOIT CURRENTLY UNUSED APRON SPACE AND TO IMPROVE CAR TRAFFIC FLOW AROUND THE TERMINAL. THE ORIGINAL TERMINAL BUILDING WILL BE DECOMMISSIONED, PARTIALLY PRESERVED (THE ORIGINAL SATELLITE PIERS WILL BE DESTROYED), AND MADE REDUNDANT BY THE NEW TERMINAL BEING BUILT AROUND IT, WHICH REDIRECTS ALL MAJOR TRAFFIC FLOWS AROUND THE ORIGINAL SAARINEN TERMINAL.

The TWA terminal seen from the air immediately prior to its inauguration.

Artist's sketch of the proposed TWA terminal. Originally published in The Port of New York Authority press release, Monday 21 February 1955.

JFK

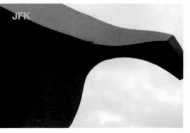

JFK

JFK

JFK

JFK

DULLES INTERNATIONAL AIRPORT, OPENED IN 1962,
WAS THE FIRST CIVIL AIRPORT SPECIFICALLY DESIGNED
TO HANDLE THE INCREASING VOLUMES OF JET TRAVEL.
THE TERMINAL BUILDING IS 182 METRES LONG BUT
WAS DESIGNED TO BE EXPANDABLE TO 548 METRES.
HOWEVER, THIS OPTION HAS NEVER BEEN TAKEN UP.
A NEW TERMINAL IS CURRENTLY BEING BUILT ADJACENT
TO THE ORIGINAL TERMINAL.

IAD

IAD

PUDONG INTERNATIONAL IS LIKE DULLES ON STEROIDS. AIRPORTS WENT FROM BEING BUILT IN THE SUBURBS AT A SUBURBAN SCALE TO BECOME SUPERMODERN CITIES IN THEIR OWN RIGHT. IN THE CASE OF PUDONG, A CITY IS BEING BUILT AROUND THE AIRPORT. IT IS DIFFICULT TO KEEP UP WITH THE MASSIVE INFRASTRUCTURE IN AND AROUND THIS ENORMOUS AIRPORT: RING ROADS, GAS WORKS, MAGNETIC ELEVATED TRAIN SYSTEMS, BRIDGES, POWER PLANTS, WATER PLANTS, TELECOMMUNICATIONS INFRASTRUCTURE, AND THE EXPANSION OF THE DEEP WATER PORT NEARBY. THE RECENTLY OPENED AIRPORT IS ALREADY UNDER RE-DEVELOPMENT AS PHASE TWO EXPANDS THE RUNWAY SYSTEM, TERMINAL BUILDINGS AND INCREASES THE AIRPORT'S CURRENT CAPACITY FROM 20 TO A POTENTIAL 80 MILLION PASSENGERS.

PVG

PVG

登机桥 23

ALCMA

PVG

PVG

PATTERN: BODIES AND MOTION IN A NETWORKED WORLD

WITHIN THE GLASS GROUNDSCRAPERS THAT DOMINATE CONTEMPORARY AIRPORT DESIGN, ONLY OUR THOUGHTS MOVE IN PRIVATE. OUR BAGGAGE, OUR BODIES AND OUR MOVEMENTS ARE ALL PART OF AN ALL-ENCOMPASSING SPECTACLE. VISIBLE TO EVERYBODY, WE DISAPPEAR INTO THE MULTIPLE MATRICES OF THE AIRPORT. PACKETED AND PROCEDURALISED, THE CONTEMPORARY AIR TRAVELLER NAVIGATES THE LOGISTICAL NETWORK ARCHITECTURE OF THE SUPERMODERN WORLD.

ONE SUCH WAY THAT OUR BODIES ARE BECOMING INTEGRATED INTO NETWORKS OF EVERYDAY LIFE IS THROUGH THE USE OF BIOMETRIC SYSTEMS OF RETINA SCANNING AND DIGITAL FINGERPRINTING THAT ARE NOW BEING UNCONTROVERSIALLY INTRODUCED AT THE AIRPORT UNDER THE AEGIS OF SECURITY AND EFFICIENT TRAFFIC MANAGEMENT. PART PASSENGER, PART LOGISTICAL PROBLEM, PART TERRORIST THREAT, THE CITIZEN OF AVIOPOLIS IS A SERIES OF PATTERN MATCHES IN THE EXPANDING DATABASES OF EVERYDAY LIFE.

"WHEN A BODY IS IN MOTION, IT DOES NOT COINCIDE WITH ITSELF. IT COINCIDES WITH ITS OWN TRANSITION: ITS OWN VARIATION."
BRIAN MASSUMI

It all started so innocently, so optimistically – or so it seemed. At the dedication ceremony of the International Arrivals Terminal in 1957 of the seemingly forever incomplete New York International Airport, James T Pyle, Administrator of Civil Aeronautics, remarked:

> Standing here before this new open door to our nation, I wonder: Will not these great international buildings contribute to a peaceful world? Can war ever again begin among men wise enough and strong enough to build this kind of a living monument to peaceful commerce? Can we not welcome through these portals visitors from all nations, and use these great buildings as a symbol of our desire to be friendly to all the people of all the world?[1]

From the very beginning of commercial jet aviation, the airport was envisioned as an open door – the portal to a new global geography of connection between people and nation states. The straight lines of the sixteenth century Mercator Projection could now be rewritten to a specifically capitalist logic in which a unified system of commerce would smooth over the frictions of cultural difference and the relative histories of particular places. In a mode that we could shorthand as 'American', money was going to make it all right. Thus begins the story of another *fin de millennium* global network: the Jet Age.

The first iteration of the arrivals terminal at New York International was touchingly inadequate for the task ahead. Its architecture imagined a more polite and rarefied form of traffic than was actually to occur. The immigration section for instance, had a series of functional but discrete interview rooms – more like a doctor's surgery than the mammoth processing counters we have today. Airports of the Jet Age were modernist monuments to a strangely cosy future, unlike the monumental steel and glass people pipes of today. In its infant state, the network had looser connections. The introduction of commercial jet services in 1959 changed all that. Bigger, faster, cheaper. Traffic increased in scale, volume, and frequency and the modest portal expanded to the point where geo-national borders warped out of orbit. A world of territorial borders morphed into a world of global patterns.

Some of these patterns are visible – like the precise geometry of runway lights at night or the miniaturised interlocking shapes of in-flight meals. Others appear more random, but are as predictable as the paths that planes travel overhead. Still other patterns are difficult to see – we are too caught up in them to notice – but they guide our behaviour and control our movement all the same. In a networked world, these patterns offer techniques for duplication, convergence and extension. Airports connect one thing to another entirely different thing by this process of meshing patterns. The airport is full of patterns that operate in every possible dimension and on every conceivable scale.

The concertina folds of the air-bridge expand to embrace the plane on the apron, the transiting passenger sees an arrow and a familiar pictogram and behaves accordingly. Within the huge glass concourses of contemporary airports, a familiarity emerges that is both tedious in experience and sublime in its promise. As we move through the transparent corridors of the supermodern airport, exhilarating panoramas unfold before us. Exotic livery of distant corporations press against the terminal's biosphere skin, while people from every place and every time zone move purposefully around us. It is a sublime spectacle of possibility that we never quite manage to apprehend totally. The fixed point of the horizon gives way to the shifting positions of a particular kind of navigation that is based on movement rather than vision. The interesting thing to note is that airports share this feature with all networks. As Steven Shaviro says of the web, "its possibilities are so vast and yet so tantalisingly incomplete, that I must get involved with it in depth".[2]

The Network Inside-out: from Optics to Haptics

Within the monumental spaces of global transit, the promise of an actual elsewhere has never seemed so present or available. The transparency of the glass groundscrapers (like the ones you find at Kansai or Pudong) offers a seemingly unmediated spectacle of movement. Visible to all, only our thoughts move in private (though soon neuroscience and brain imaging may put an end to even that). Our baggage, our bodies, our movements are all part of an encompassing spectacle. In public queues we see the most intimate of moments: a young man being pulled aside and questioned by security; anxious travellers compulsively patting their pockets for wallets and passports; an elderly woman repacking her bag to fit the weight allowance. Visible to everybody, we disappear into the matrix of the airport. As we navigate through alphanumeric landscapes of Gate 76 and Counter B, we also 'toggle' between national and corporate zones by passing a series of checkpoints. Flesh to image to code and back again, security machines scan us both inside and out. Our bio-data is uploaded into the database. In the glazed spectacle of all this movement, we are both inspired and instructed. A vision of global possibilities is offered to the traveller, but it is a vision that when accessed transforms into the protocols of code. In other words, when we begin to move through the networks we stop being spectators and become navigators in every sense. When you are in transit, you are heading somewhere. Your itinerary, not your location, structures your experience. When passengers walk an airport they are navigating the material embodiment of information architecture. At the airport this architecture is expressed through folds, frames and patterns at those threshold points where the binaries of inside/outside, public/private, movement/stasis once ruled. For instance, how does inside/outside really work when you can be inside the plane and still outside the terminal building, when you can be inside the airport but not yet in the country, and so on? Borders of all kinds become refined into series of connections and processes.

At the airport we move from point to point (immigration to departure gate), from sign to sign (Gate 76 to Seat 43K), link to link, and node to node, never really seeing the end – just new destinations. Quite literally immersed in the networks of global movement, we are, as Deleuze and Guattari would say, "lost without landmarks in smooth space".[3] No longer in the optical space of landscape, we are in a network-transit space of pure connection.

Transit space might be full of visual media (like signs), but we experience them via the processes of movement, which necessarily changes our vision. As we extend ourselves across networks we no longer see the big picture. We constantly seem to interact with fragments. Our involvement with networks is so close that our vision becomes more tactile or 'haptic' rather than merely optical.[4] Or, put another way, we don't just see the patterns – we move through them. And it is through movement that the patterns form. Ubiquitous, invisible and operational patterns enable one system to lock into another and multiply, creating patterns in connection that operate across multiple modes and multiple scales, from the very small of biotech to the monumental scale of an international airport. As we move about the airport we distribute ourselves through the network by logging into different information systems and redirecting ourselves into different flows. Integrated into the matrix, all our senses are deployed as we move through the networks of transit – following signs, drinking the franchised coffee, having government officials swipe our databases and swab our computers. The very idea that we, embodied creatures, can move in the networks of everyday life by fragmentation raises certain questions about what kind of body we may have become. For instance, if we can move simultaneously in multiple modes, then what kind of body is it that can exist in constant variation? What kind of new relations cohere in a world where one is necessarily fractured in order to stay in the loop of everyday life? Finally, how does power operate through these new relations of bodies-to-themselves in the complex cross-patterning of networked life?

As any crime boss, think tank lobbyist, or CEO will tell you, networks are not merely technical: they are political. The patterns that cohere across any network directly impact upon the things that move. It is not about where you are on a global grid or in a social hierarchy. The important thing is the networks you have access to. This is

not to deny the capacity of power to exclude, or to suggest that geopolitics do not still have devastating consequences for people. Rather it is to assert that another type of power emerges in a networked world in which space is figured through flow, frequency and capacity rather than through some kind of organic relation to lived territories and nation states. As networks increase, everything becomes nodal – like a series of terminals in a computer network. Spaces converge, multi-task and duplicate. Schiphol Airport, for instance, is a seamless multi-platform transport hub and a major European mall at the same time. In spaces like Schiphol where the demands of a global economy based on transnational movement supersede the dying ideologies of nation states, it becomes impossible to use barriers and walls to contain a sense of discrete or different spaces (even if conservative Western governments want to believe this could still be true.) As Brian Massumi notes, "containment has more to do with the patterning of exits and entries across thresholds than with the impermeabilities of boundaries".[5]

This patterning across entries and exits as a form of control operates through many dimensions. For example, traffic management is based on patterns inferred from a range of data that turns the seeming chaos of traffic into a series of temporally and spatially coordinated flows. Lights are programmed differently for peak hours so as to keep the patterns of traffic smooth and predictable. Bar coding enables a precision in dynamic micro-managing that is increasingly being applied to our bodies. At multiple levels, we are becoming collectively integrated into informational processes that are open to biotechnical forms of regulation. Techniques like gene therapy, forensic science or biometrics are being pioneered in medicine, criminology and security. Fields that once molded the individual through bodily confinement and observation are dispersing and converging into the regimes of logistics and control. Bodies and machines measure each other – scanning each other constantly, calibrating, adjusting and entwining in all kinds of new biotechnical rhythms. Simultaneously mass and singular, user and demographic, identity and pattern match, a new body navigates the data-masses of modern life. This new body is both body and life, or as Foucault put it, "life in general – with the body as one pole and the population on the other".[6]

In a world of control access systems people are no longer 'interpreted' by moral standards but are 'authenticated' at a series of thresholds. Flesh, body and name are matched simultaneously to info-body and database – a body of electronic traces, image archives and credit card purchases, social security information, and travel itineraries, each hooked into another body (of information). Thus, on one hand, we are dealing with flesh bodies, while on the other, we are concerned with a pattern match. Or as Deleuze notes: "We're no longer dealing with a duality of mass and individual. Individuals become 'dividuals' and masses become sample, data, markets, or banks."[7] An individual is supposedly something that cannot be divided, and yet techniques that attempt to know and to control the individual by measuring them are proliferating in multiple fields. Measurement enables 'one' to divide across infinite planes and dimensions and to reconfigure endlessly.

If the control and commodification of mobility and access has made our haptic relations to space more obvious, then different techniques are required to know this new and perhaps more complex body that has subsequently emerged. Visual profiling – the apprehension of a being-in-totality – is costly, time consuming and famously inaccurate. In a world where communities are not necessarily formed by shared blood or soil but through itineraries and subscription plans, e-lists, TV, evangelical religions and other such networked event spaces, its difficult to know someone by their physical outline. It is easier to know them by their patterns. And so 'code', itself a term that resides in so many fields of action – from codex to rule, from military ciphers to genetic science – evolves again and connects meaning to machines, bodies to hardware, mixing the hard, the soft and the ineffable of the world.

Soft and Hard: Biometrics

Both Schiphol and Heathrow airports began trialing biometric systems before September 11. Countless others have started using such systems since. Anyone from a visa-category country wanting to travel to the USA from 2004 or Britain from 2005 must have a biometric encrypted in their travel documents. And so, levered into position through the politics of crisis and fear, biometrics quietly moves out of the spaces of exception into the open circuits of capital and regulation, becoming part of the information architecture of everyday life. Anyone who resists patching their body into a global network of tracking and control will simply not gain access.

Biometric systems realise visual representations, such as the complex pattern of striations in the iris or the contours of the palm, and render them as numeric representations (statistical variables). The body that was dispersed through abstraction can now be pulled together in different formations due to the transformative power of algorithms. The increase of biometric technologies (along with DNA mapping and a whole range of biotech industries) seems to signal a new development in the very ancient 'sympathetic magic' of mimesis – a shift away from the visual to a more intimate form of contact based on manipulating a variable databody (and not on representing the body as an image). Biometrics at the airport is about modulation rather than mediation.

Patterns quite literally set precedents that must be followed. Through the techniques of measurement and duplication, life is flattened onto one ontological plane, approximated at neural net processing speed and controlled according to the algorithms of probabilistic statistics. With the rise of biometric systems of control access, life becomes quite literally a pattern match, and identity politics starts looking very weird. No longer just concerned with gross categories like race, gender, sexuality and the like, the apparatuses of state capture have gone cellular and the biological caesuras that race once ensured can be refined into other areas. As Foucault notes "the distinction among races, the hierarchy of races, the fact that certain races are described as good and others, in contrast are described as inferior: all this is a way of fragmenting the field of the biological that power controls".[8]

The primary binary of self/other – a feature of code, but not necessarily of life – became a ruthless heuristic for explaining the complex ecologies of the world. Categories of race, gender, religion, sexuality all deconstructed as limiting codifications in a signifying realm, were, however, not wiped off the map (by either ethnic cleansers in a material way, or by anti-essentialists in a conceptual way). With the introduction of technologies that can match code to a non-transferable singularity such as the body, categories were repositioned on the map into more patrolled territory. The fluidity of identity has moved beyond issues of post colonial hybridity, queer play and e-performance. Identity is now so fluid as to be formless – it's a pattern that coheres momentarily and then dissolves. Any form of identity is necessarily regulatory; one set of attributes are recognised and privileged, others are excluded. Identity is actually quite odd to think about from a network perspective. Identity, as a term, denies the connectedness of the network. Identity in a biometric world of code is not a psychic belonging, a negotiation over beliefs, rights and power. It is now a data match fractured across multiple programmes in n-dimensional space: identity becomes a roaming oscillation, looking for a pattern match in a machine. In a world of constant movement where global migrations and mass media have troubled the once easy attribution of race with otherness, regulative technologies move beyond the skin to code life itself: everyone is captured in this net.

In some strange way, although the body (and its ability to move) is what seems most at stake on the threshold when access is either allowed or denied, it is at this moment that the body seems most irrelevant to the abstraction of the biometric. When identity is matched, the body is always out of position, so to speak. It is freeze-framed. The variations – the various 'shimmerings' of a body – are

reprogrammed into an algorithm. Thus unique aspects of life are now a selected assignation of variables, numerically represented and available for all kinds of substitutions into all kinds of areas. Life is now available to the database. It has become a potential across a series of networked ecologies.

Traffic Management

Biometrics is part of traffic management. Traffic management is part of security and security is part of service. The increasingly transient nature of everyday life forces the stability of disciplinary regimes into logistical micro-managing. The bio-political mechanisms of forecasts and statistical elements, of risk management and regulation are part of this logic. Biometrics is yet another way in which the flows of life are increasingly captured and reassembled through 'stop-go' technologies that don't work through signification but instantiate us straight into informational sequences.

Biometrics is concerned with keeping people in or out: of buildings, of websites, of countries. It is a method of controlling the chaos of movement and of protecting capital from contagion. It streamlines the flow for those with the right password. Life weaves across many ontological consistencies and reproduces itself in multiple modes. Connected across time and space through different modes of symbiosis and contagion, the borders between lifeforms shift and evolve. In a world of transit, movement becomes highly regulated by networks in which public and private are almost indistinguishable, in which individual and mass cohere through statistically rendered singularities – in other words, a pattern match.

A series of paradoxes emerge within the evolution of digitised and cross-platform biometrics: movement occurs through capture; sight occurs without vision; individuals are divided within themselves. If something that is apparently illogical not only exists but actually thrives in the world, then either something is up with our theory of reality or the logic of the world is changing. Either way, new relations are made visible by the emergence of new control techniques that give some insight into the issues of power in a networked world. They give us a sense of what new languages might be required to articulate the coming global urbanism.

The world really has changed since radio, telegrams, television and aviation propelled us into network space/time. Navigating the mutant geometries of modern life invokes a strange sensuality, captured and thoughtless, free while anonymous, neither here nor there, telematic and fractal. As we pass through the thresholds of networked life, we become an organism of that ecology: a potential that could go anywhere controlled through the regulatory but inventive techniques of patterns.

1   Civil Aviation was then under the auspices of United States Department of Commerce.

2   Shaviro, Steven, *Connected: What it Means to Live in the Network Society*, Mineapolis: University of Minnesota Press, 2003, p. 6.

3   Deleuze, Gilles and Guattari, Felix, *A Thousand Plateaus: Capitalism and Schizophrenia*, Brian Massumi trans, London: Athlone Press, p. 493.

4   For a discussion of haptic space as a form of close vision see Deleuze and Guattari, *A Thousand Plateaus*, 1987.

5   Massumi, Brian, *Parables for the Virtual: Movement, Affect, Sensation*, Durham: Duke University Press, 2002, p. 85.

6   Foucault, Michel, "Seminar of 17 March 1976" in *Society Must be Defended*, New York: Picador, 1996 p. 253.

7   Deleuze, Gilles, "Postscript on Control Societies", in *Negotiations*, New York: Columbia University Press, 1995, p. 180.

8   Foucault, "Seminar", p. 255.

Airport signage organises space into controlled flows. In this sense, the airport provides laboratory conditions for a consideration of the distinctions that still hold between the objects of architecture and the processes of interactive media. The airport clearly demonstrates the need for a shared conceptual language between media and architecture. An airport is not just a building, nor is it just a process. It is an event space – defined not just in terms of its behaviours in specific times and places, but in terms of its virtualised relations of continuity and chance.

The distinction between the building
and its signs, between the text and the
territory, becomes indistinct through the
act of traversal in these complex multi-
dimensional spaces. In an airport the
passenger is a navigator more than a
reader. Scenes are made and unmade.
Universes open up and close down in
a series of architectural and semiotic
'reveals', we move through a map/space –
as politically charged as any map, and
as banal as everyday life.

KIX

As we move from point to point, we come together as different data configurations at each threshold. If we do not follow the procedures, if our bodies don't match with the right sequence, we will be denied access. No longer just the subject of the optical technologies of surveillance, we are now patched directly into the network. The machines no longer just look – they are so close that they now touch us.

Information architecture is materially expressed through folds, frames and patterns where the oppositions of interiority/exteriority, public/private, movement/stasis have been refined into series of connections and processes.

SIN

KIX

KIX

国際線到着 International Arrivals

MSP

Infohubs have become an essential part of transit life, where the global citizen fractures into multiple dimensions in order to stay in the loop of everyday life.

We may still live in one singular body, but we now also have a multitude of identities, passwords and behaviours, depending on where we are in the network.

TRANSCAPITALISM AND THE MULTIPLE ECOLOGIES OF AN AVIOPOLIS

AIRPORTS ARE 'TERRAFORMERS'. THEY LITERALLY REFORM LAND AND IN SOME CASES MAKE IT. ACROSS THE GLOBE SWAMPS TRANSMUTE INTO CONCRETE SLABS, DRAINAGE CANALS AND TERMINAL STRUCTURES AND, STARTING IN THE PACIFIC BUT HEADING WEST, AIRPORTS ARE GRADUALLY FORMING A GLOBAL ARCHIPELAGO, RISING OUT OF THE SEA ON MASSIVE PURPOSE-BUILT ISLANDS.

AIRPORTS RECONFIGURE GEOGRAPHY ACCORDING TO THE SPATIO-TEMPORAL RHYTHMS AND CROSS-MODAL STANDARDS OF GLOBAL CAPITAL, BY FLATTENING ALL DIFFERENCE INTO MANAGEABLE, MEASURABLE AND COMMODIFIABLE CONTOURS. AIRPORTS ARE GEO-MECHANICAL-DIGITAL FORMS THAT ARE CHANGING THE CONTOURS OF LAND, SEA AND SKY. TO CONSIDER THE RELATIONSHIP BETWEEN AN AIRPORT AND ITS ENVIRONS IS TO CONSIDER THE ENTWINING OF MOVEMENT, MONEY, LAND, SKY, MATTER AND INFORMATION.

"WE BUILD WORLDS, WE DON'T JUST TERRAFORM PLANETS." *TERRY PRATCHETT* [1]

Tethered to the ocean floor through a series of adjustable columns and connected to the mainland by a 3.8 kilometre truss bridge, Kansai International Airport creates a strangely geometric reef off the coast of Southern Honshu, Japan. Built on a five-square kilometre island in Osaka Bay and fed traffic and trade by the growing megacity of Kyoto-Kobe, Kansai was built to be the first 24 hour aviation hub in south east Asia.[2] Sufficiently offshore from the regulations and noise restrictions associated with local time, Kansai was designed to be a node that could operate on global time and at global scales. The terminal building is a massive steel and glass tube, over 1.7 kilometres long, wing-shaped and perpetually drenched in light. It is the epitome of a contemporary airport: a marvel of geo-engineering, a brand name architect (Renzo Piano) and an 'elsewhere aesthetic' that promises its users passage into another realm.

But regardless of its eerie other-dimensionality, Kansai is most definitely entwined into the surrounding urban landscape through rail links, road networks, through the income it generates, and through all the other infrastructure it needs and creates in order to survive as a viable global node.

Airports are not alone in this ability to weave the materialities of place into the creative abstractions of space by way of architecture. Networks cut directly across many spaces, but the airport offers exemplary conditions for thinking about connective space. Kansai is a geo-mechanical digital form, stable only in its constant instability. It is also a 'metaform' that ties together global and local traffic. A 'metastable metaform', Kansai (like all airports) changes the contours of land, sea and sky.

Airports mix multiple forms of life, matter and information into a series of new and constantly changing relations between bodies and the sky, between local landscapes and global capital. They do this by creating thresholds that enable disparate systems to meet each other. At the airport, the relatively slow and individuated systems of ground transportation meet with the faster mass systems of aviation. It is at this intersection that local urban ecologies begin to entwine with the global. The airport is a structure that is also an infrastructure. It is a structure designed for connection.

Airports invite a connective type of thinking that operates at a geological scale, and not just at the level of place, people, and time zone (which are themselves abstractions of global jet-time). Despite the fact that airports create some of the most anonymous zones in the world, it is impossible to isolate any airport from the ecology of its environs.

The ecologies we are invoking here are not limited to some idealised notion of 'nature'. As airports increasingly become metaforms, insinuating themselves into urban infrastructures and geological/botanical landscapes, we prefer a more generalised notion of ecology that recognises all manner of topological connections that may exist across a range of systems. As Felix Guattari notes in *The Three Ecologies*:

> Now more than ever, nature cannot be separated from culture; in order to comprehend the interactions between ecosystems, the mechanosphere and the social and individual universes of reference, we must learn to think transversally.[3]

The airport depends on what Alfred Whitehead would call the 'patience of the environment'. Or as Isabelle Stengers has put it, "the ethos of an organism, its specific grasping together of aspects of its environment, cannot be dissociated from its ecology".[4] The airport itself is an organism that is in a feedback loop with the environment, which is itself in a constant state of flux and change. All over the world, the energy and matter of local environments are being redirected into a global ecology that requires smooth connections for the endless circulation of commodities. Contemporary airports reconfigure their environs as a series of nodes in multiple ecologies, hooking up the local to the monumental scales of global aviation. They create worlds that exceed the capacity of contemporary urban planning.

Airports are 'terraformers'. They literally make land. They flatten difference into manageable contours, reconfiguring geography according to the spatio-temporal rhythms and cross-modal standards of global capital. This tendency to terraform is common among many modern international airports, such as Kansai, Osaka, Chek Lap Kok in Hong Kong, Pudong, Shanghai, or Sydney, Australia. Rising out of the sea, sucking up land and reforming it into platforms for planes and cars, strange geographies emerge from this meeting of car, plane, tunnel and runway. These cross-platform axes of movement create structures and shapes that breach previous logics of space.

In Foucault's later work on space and power, he began speculating about an increase of these 'other' kinds of spaces – spaces of multiplicities and cross-overs, spaces where old disciplinary distinctions (and thus old methods of control) break down.

> Perhaps our life is still governed by a certain number of oppositions that remain inviolable, that our institutions and practices have not yet dared to break down. These are the oppositions that we regard as simple givens: for example between private space and public space, between family space and social space, between cultural space and useful space, between the space of leisure and the space of work.[5]

At the airport these distinctions are collapsing to create spaces in which the polis is both a logistical node in a global network and a mythical place of promise. Old distinctions between private and public, leisure and work, open and closed, global and local, complete and incomplete, fold in on each other to create spaces of multiple relations. The airport is an 'other space' – a real space that is linked to numerous other types of spaces, contradicting and inverting the sites which it connects. It is not a place that has a defined border, but instead dissolves into a series of modalities that blend into the city – the motorway, the airport rail link, aircraft noise limits, regenerated buffer zones, and the navigational beacons that are fretted across the city landscape.

No airport has an absolute limit. They make runways in the middle of bays, their sonic footprints can be heard for miles, their legislative reign stretches across nations. The airport is a world of looping horizons. It unfurls out over the city and insinuates itself into the daily activities of the dispersing world. In its endless grasping of the environment, old futures are abandoned and new ones appear.

In Neal Stephenson's science fiction novel *The Diamond Age*, John Hackworth (neo-Victorian and engineer for the omnipotent corporation Imperial Tectonics) witnesses the creation of a purpose-built coral island reef, which bursts out of the depths of the ocean.

> Viewed through the dark surface of the Pacific, it was like watching an explosion through a pane of shattered glass. It reminded him of pouring a jet of heavy cream into coffee and watching it rebound from the bottom of the cup in a turbulent fractal bloom that solidified just as it dashed against the surface.[6]

The same exhilaration and anxiety about terraforming evident in Stephenson's fictional universe is also at work in the design and operation of supermodern airports. After decades of land clearing, swamp draining, reef building and road building, the bays, artificial islands and coastlines that constitute many airports are barely recognisable from their former contours, and yet as both Marc Augé notes and Neal Stephenson hints in the passage above, non-places never really erase the particularities and politics of place.[7]

If Kansai presents the tendency to build new worlds out of 'nowhere', its precursor must be Tokyo's Narita, 64 kilometres out from the centre of Tokyo and situated on compulsorily acquired farmland. In the 1970s Narita was the focus of sustained protests by locals, which stalled the 'completion' of the airport until 2002, when its second runway eventually opened (albeit 300 metres short because of the local farmers who still oppose all forms of airport expansion). Since its inception Narita has been a focal point of political controversy and local anger.

Similar political struggles occurred in the southern Pacific at Sydney International when, in 1994, after 25 years of building into Botany Bay more of the bay was dredged to make room for a 2,438 metre runway, situated entirely on reclaimed land. There were also countless controversies over the construction of the new Chep Lak Kok Airport in Hong Kong (no stranger to the idea of reclaiming land) as the once holiday island of Lantau was utterly reformed into an international movement machine. Each of these expansions reinitiates yet another debate about the nature of global and local borders, as beaches are buried under runways, bridges are built, roads are expanded and the smell of avgas mingles with the diesel fumes of increasing freight.

No airport is without controversy. They are always encroaching on the residences below, rearranging the economies of communities and altering the intertidal, marine or avian ecologies.

The airport pulls everything tighter together even as it seems to be pulling it all apart. It is a site where all kinds of transgressions across discrete spaces, times and systems occur – in which the very latest of air guidance control systems mingle with ancient wetlands and marine ecologies. Contemporary airports create 'techno-cultural miasmas' and new modes of life. In his evocative discussion of the important role corruption and contagion play in the cycles of life, Michael Taussig reminds us that the ancient Greek word for contagion, *miasma*, arises from a transgression.

> Finding our way through mud and mangroves I become aware there is no border between land and sea. What exists is not a coast but a blur. The mangroves claw at the mud, like me, matter falling through time with a strange comfort in a sucking motion where being coagulates in a unity of sticky shadows. This morass is definitely the long sought in-between of sludge rising and falling with the tide, home to all manner of life forms, the lunar zone of rot and decay in whose slow, eternal rhythms, clouds of shrimp waft and crabs hide.[8]

Many airports seem to flower in the rotting and seemingly most unusable spaces on earth: Idlewild, Pudong, Sydney, Changi and

Kansai are just a few. In the age of mobility machines, all kinds of transgressive co-minglings occur. The noise of jets overwhelms the blare of the TV in suburban homes. The airport and its city become indistinguishable.

The airport is a seeping miasma of control spaces and logistical architecture that is woven into the everyday life of the city. This is a city of movement, where traffic and architecture hum in synergistic flows and at different rhythms; and yet everything is geared towards greater integration and the smooth imperatives of transcapitalism. Decentralised and deterritorialised, the city is rewritten according to a global logic of connection. In the case of China, nation, state, and economy have almost seamlessly merged in an endless series of key development zones and free trade areas that enact the notion of the networked global city in the most literal of ways. In the current Five Year Plan, China has committed to build or redevelop 41 airports.

If you build it, they will come: the case of Pudong

Pudong Airport, 30 kilometres east of Shanghai, is a glass and steel behemoth rising out the sodden and sinking earth of the 'Pudong New Area'. Currently in Phase One of its development, Pudong has one mega-barn terminal building and one runway. In this capacity it processes 20 million passenger movements a year. When Pudong reaches Phase Four in 2010, it will have four runways, four mammoth terminals and will process an estimated 80 million passenger movements a year, making it potentially the busiest airport in the world. In the meantime a new mega-city will have grown around it. On the delta plane formed by the convergence of the Yangste and Huang Po Rivers into the East China Sea, dead-straight boulevards and looping on/off ramps slice through a once rural landscape. In the 'opening up' of China, the land has 'grown' infrastructure for the oncoming traffic on a scale never before seen. Pudong is growing in every dimension and at all manner of speeds: all around the airport half-built elevated highways jut into the air; a 'high tech' magnetic

elevation train sits still in its station; the port nearby, already the fifth busiest in the world, is busy building more deepwater facilities. Closer towards Shanghai, a multitude of discrete development zones (Lujiazui Finance and Trade Zone, the Waigaoqiao Free Trade Zone, the Zhangjiang Hi-Tech Park, and the Huaxia Cultural Tourism Zone) grow in between an expanding system of highways that snake across the Pudong New Area into south eastern China. In addition to extending port and airport facilities, a third 'infoport' is being developed, cabling fibre optic networks and broadband into the metro area network known as Shanghai/Pudong.

This fracturing and cross-connecting of discrete space (inherent to the segmented, networked urban structures of Pudong) is indicative of an urbanity that is coming to many places around the world. These new zones are dispersed across discrete functional spaces and operate under multiple jurisdictions. For instance, Lujiazui Finance and Trade Zone is optimistically envisaged as the new 'Asian Wall Street' where international finance institutions will congregate. A concentration of high-tech businesses will emerge in the Jinqiao Export Processing Zone. The Waigaoqiao Free Trade Zone and the harbour area will perform integrated services to process the 'free trade'. The Zhangjiang Hi-Tech Park will become a base for the development of bio-pharmaceutics and micro-electronics.

However, in its current state, Pudong seems strangely empty: it is all infrastructure, denser in potential than actuality. But as Pudong grows urban matter extending up into wacky and sublime skyscrapers, and out into a expanding highway system, the complex interactions of geology, politics, and economic ideologies speed up exponentially. The infrastructure rushes out to grasp 200 million people who will soon live within a three hour drive of the Pudong/Shanghai delta.

Already, the smog in the Shanghai air makes it hard to discern the transition between land and sky. This seems typical of how we are reshaping the planet to match our miasmic conceptual worlds. If the marker of the modernist city is the high-rise, in which a vertical aesthetic anxiously asserts autonomy and separation in a world that increasingly demands connection and flow, then the airport is the emblem of the transcapitalist city of today. Smearing out over the landscape (including the sky above) it turns mobility into a productive force that continues to demonstrate its ability to reshape modern urbanity.

What is form when everything is movement?

> We treat each [of them] as a thing rather than as a progress, forgetting that the very permanence of their form is only the outline of a movement.
> Henri Bergson[9]

The airport is a transcapitalist ecology that is sustained through interaction with other ecosystems, each with their own logic, rhythm and scale. From the local politics of aircraft noise to the geopolitics of trade, once an airport is built, whole landscapes (geographical, social and political) mutate on a monumental scale to accommodate mass mobility.

The runway, apron systems and the terminal buildings are only a fragment of the airport's impact on the environs around it. Other flow infrastructures like highways, bridges and tunnels virally replicate around airports, as do ancillary businesses, such as global logistics companies, airline service providers, hotels and conferencing facilities. As movement becomes a major urban organiser, the airport stretches out and entwines all aspects of life into its rhythms and procedures.

The way you need to think about your life gets complex when you encounter the airport. A state identity is raised through a passport, a strange temporality emerges on your ticket as you realise that you will arrive the day before you left; or as you pack your bags you begin thinking about weather patterns in another hemisphere. Life fractures into different geographies, the 'here' and the 'now', the 'there' and the 'then', the possible and the actual all begin to loop into each other. It is hardly surprising that a space that is utterly about relationality would invoke multiple modes of spatiality within it. In other words, an airport is a place without a place or a space within a space – or both. Such a space is both open and closed. It is isolated and yet at the same time connected. It carries with its structures the remnant features of genealogies of a past and anticipates a future.

In a transcapitalist world where movement is everything it is perhaps no surprise that the next great experiment in terraforming will be an 'Airport City', an artificial island 10 km in diameter in the North Sea off the coast of Holland. The new Schiphol Airport, being developed by Rem Koolhaas' Office for Metropolitan Architecture, will be connected to the mainland by high-speed rail and a freeway. Devised to be a new hub for Europe, a 24 hour airport and a fully functioning autonomous city, this airport city could be both a floating fortress and a major traffic hub – it will most likely be both. The airport is a place where everything seems separated – but really it is connected. This is because the airport operates across so many qualitatively distinct levels that its operational logic is a 'translogic'. Its complex topology of connections, movements and transformations can only be understood by looking at movement.

So what is the form of something that is never still? If an airport has a form it is that of a dance. Choreography incorporates the monumental and the minute, the very fast and the rather slow, the concrete and the mythical into a series of movements that continually cross-reference and activate each other. This suggests that we need to think of the airport as a topology of relations continuously folding and unfolding in and out of a multitude of dimensions. The airport is a modulation that shapes the earth – and shape the earth the airport will. It must build new worlds.

As an integral part of the networking of the world into the space of flows, the airport is implicated into two seemingly contradictory trajectories. One is a course of unexplored potentials as new modalities cross-fertilise and commingle; the other is locked into a particularly unthinking beat in which everyone gets in-synch without ever wondering if they're being "anaesthetised by a collective feeling of pseudo-eternity".[10]

In *The Three Ecologies*, Felix Guattari refers to the need for an ecosophy where individuals must become both more united and increasingly different. The problem of politics at the moment is that 'united' appears to mean 'think the same' or 'do the same'. As September 11 shows us, the networks that bring us together do not necessarily entail global homogeneity. That is why they are so anxiously patrolled. And yet, at the airport/mall/parking-lot/police-state/transit-hub/city-of-the-future, multiple possibilities are closed down in the interests of efficiency and security. We can only hope that this will not last, that the virtual will not be completely quashed, and that the new possibilities so fundamental to flight will not be erased.

1   Pratchett, Terry, *Strata*, London: Corgi, 1988.
2   Borja, Jordi and Castells, Manuel, "The impact of globalisation on the spatial and social structure of cities", in *Local and Global: The Management of Cities in the Information Age*, EarthScan: New York, 1997.
3   Guattari, Felix, *The Three Ecologies,* London: The Athlone Press, 2000, p. 43.
4   Stengers, Isabelle, "Whitehead and the Laws of Nature", in *Salzburger Theologische Zeitschrift*, 3 Issue 2, 1999, pp 193-206.
5   Foucault, Michel, "Of Other Spaces", *Diacritics* Vol. 16, No. 1, 1986, p. 24
6   Stephenson, Neal, *The Diamond Age*, London: Bantam, 2000, p. 14.
7   Augé, Marc, *Non-places: An Introduction to an Anthropology of Supermodernity*, J Howe trans, London: Verso, 1995.
8   Taussig, Michael, "Miasma", in Gay Hawkins and Steven Muecke eds, *Culture and Waste*, Maryland: Rowman & Littlefield, 2003.
9   Bergson, Henri, *Creative Evolution,* Arthur Mitchell trans, London: Dover Books, 1907, p. 128.
10 Guattari, *The Three Ecologies,* p. 25.

Islands

Constructed on a purpose built five square kilometre island, Kansai engineers the regulated systems of aviation into the substrata of the earth through a series of adjustable columns that jack the island up as it subsides into the seabed. The island is connected to the mainland by a 3.8 kilometre bridge has an upper deck for motor vehicles and a lower deck for trains.

Local Conflict

Looking at the strangely precise yet chaotic geometries of cities from the air, one realises there are no static forms – just the outlines of movement. Narita Airport has been under construction for nearly 40 years. When the airport opened in 1978 it had only one runway as local farmers refused to give up the land for the proposed second runway. The second runway was finally completed in 2002. Construction on new terminal structures is ongoing.

SYD

Airports are metastable – they are stable in their instability. One aspect of this stable instability is that airports are constantly upgrading. All of the 15 airports we visited for this study had either recently completed an upgrade or were undergoing an upgrade.

Many airports create spaces of 'local colour' or themed environments within the anonymous 'anywhereness' of the international terminal. Singapore's Changi Airport is a major innovator in creating themed landscapes within the terminal environs. Changi is full of ponds, waterfalls and specialist gardens, known as 'The Nature Trail'.

Growing Infrastructure

In the 'opening up' of China, the land has 'grown' infrastructure for the oncoming traffic on a scale never before seen. Currently in Phase One of its development (one terminal building and one runway), Pudong processes 20 million passenger movements a year. When it reaches Phase Four in 2010, it will have four runways, four terminals and will process an estimated 80 million passenger movements a year.

SYD JFK PVG

PVG PVG PVG

119

SYD

Growing Airspace

Sydney Airport is a medium-sized
airport (it processes around 23 million
passengers a year) and is located only
ten kilometres from the centre of the
city. It exemplifies how the global
networks of airports are entwined with
local geography, demography and
politics. Sydney Airport is currently
operating at capacity, with very little
room for further expansion, the decision
to build a second airport is continually
postponed as each new site selected is
met with vigorous community protest.

SYD

SYD

SYD

In the 1960s, Sydney Airport extended the main north-south runway (16R/34L) over two kilometres into the bay, first in 1963, to accommodate 707s and DC3s, and again, in 1969, to handle the increased size and weight of 747s.

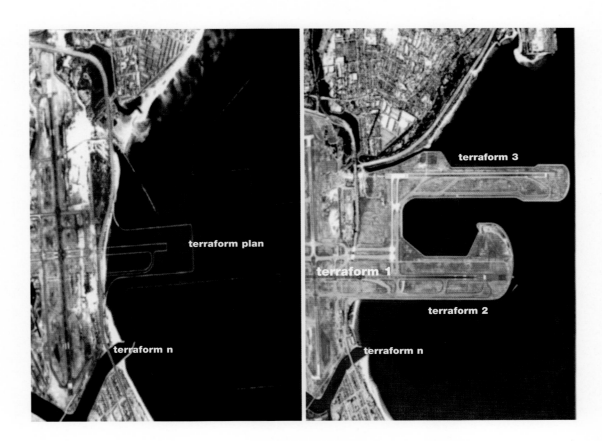

terraform 3

terraform plan

terraform 1

terraform 2

terraform n

terraform n

AIRPORT SEMIOLOGY

SIGNS MEAN THINGS. THEY ALSO DO THINGS. FOR INSTANCE, A LOT OF SIGNS AT THE AIRPORT NOT ONLY 'MAKE MEANING' THAT CAN BE INTERPRETED, THEY ALSO ISSUE DIRECT COMMANDS THAT MUST BE OBEYED. OFTEN, SIGNS WORK WITH MATTER AND DIRECTLY CONTROL MOVEMENT AND BEHAVIOUR. THESE SIGNS, LIKE LINKS AND BUTTONS ON COMPUTER INTERFACES, CONJOIN SEMIOTIC AND MATERIAL FLOWS IN A WORLD WHERE THE INFORMATIONAL AND THE MATERIAL INCREASINGLY STREAM THROUGH EACH OTHER. THE AIRPORT IS FULL OF SIGNS THAT DELIVER 'MESSAGES' THAT WE NEVER INTERPRET OR QUESTION, BECAUSE THEY DON'T DELIVER INFORMATION. THEY DELIVER ACCESS, SOMETHING WE ARE GRANTED OR DENIED. OUR AIRPORT SEMIOLOGY DOCUMENTS HOW AIRPORTS DELIVER MESSAGES ABOUT THE CONTEMPORARY ART OF LOGISTICS.

A provisional taxonomy of airport logistics

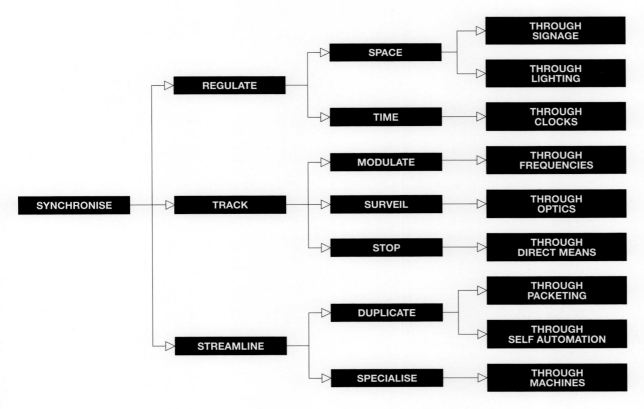

This diagram describes just one part of a complex system by which airports synchronise multiple units (like people, cars, baggage and planes) with each other. This system of synchronisation has three basic sub-systems: regulation (the means by which systems are unified and controlled); tracking (the means by which units are identified while in movement); and streamlining (the means by which movements and exchanges are made as efficient as possible). Each of these sub-systems can be broken down further. For instance, space can be regulated through the use of directional and locational signage, it can also be regulated through lighting, which enables the airport to be open for business at any time.

The following taxonomy is a fragment of a much larger and more complex system. Like any taxonomy it could be recast to privilege other relations. For our current purposes we want to highlight just some of the differences within the various systems of control at the airport.

SYNCHRONISE/STREAMLINE/
SPECIALISE/THROUGH MACHINES

SYNCHRONISE/REGULATE/ SPACE/THROUGH SIGNAGE

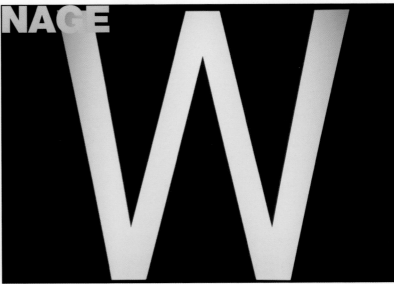

SYNCHRONISE/REGULATE/SPACE/ THROUGH LIGHTING

航空会社 Airline		便名 Flight		カウンタ 備考 Counter Remarks		変更 Will Depart
日本航空		JL 713	E-F	通関中		
日本アジア航空		EG 233	E.G	通関中		
中国国際航空		CA 1922	E.G	通関中		
エールフランス		AF 291	E.G	通関中		12:35
日本航空		JL 435	E-F	通関中		12:35
中国東方航空		MU 5774	E.G	通関中		
中国東方航空		MU 516	E.G			
全日空		NH 5155	H			
日本航空		JL 963	E-F			

SYNCHRONISE/REGULATE/TIME/
THROUGH CLOCKS

SYNCHRONISE/TRACK/MODULATE/ THROUGH FREQUENCIES

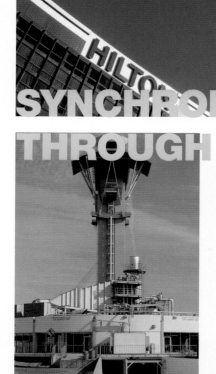

SYNCHRONISE/TRACK/SURVEIL/ THROUGH OPTICS

SYNCHRONISE/TRACK/STOP/THROUGH DIRECT MEANS

SYNCHRONISE/STREAMLINING/DUPLICATE/THROUGH PACKETING

SYNCHRONISE/REGULATE/SPACE/ THROUGH SELF AUTOMATION

AIRPORT GEOMETRIES

THE AVIOPOLIS, THE NETWORKED AND DISPERSED CITY OF THE AIR, OPERATES RATHER DIFFERENTLY THAN A METROPOLIS. THIS CITY HAS A DIFFERENT COMMAND OVER SPACE THAN THE CITY OF SKYLINES. THE AVIOPOLIS TURNS MOBILITY AND CONNECTION INTO A PRODUCTIVE FORCE THAT PRODUCES VALUE AND IN THE PROCESS RESHAPES A CITY AND ITS INFRASTRUCTURE. STRANGE GEOMETRIES EMERGE AT THE CROSSROADS OF MULTIPLE SYSTEMS OF MOVEMENT AS CROSS-PLATFORM AXES OF MOVEMENT CREATE STRUCTURES AND SHAPES THAT BREACH PREVIOUS LOGICS OF SPACE.

KIX

LAX

3F

MIA

SYD

MIA

LHR

LAX

LHR

"Stop snoring" "Sorry"

Airbus A340. The quietest long-haul cabin in the sky

JCDecaux

LHR

AMS

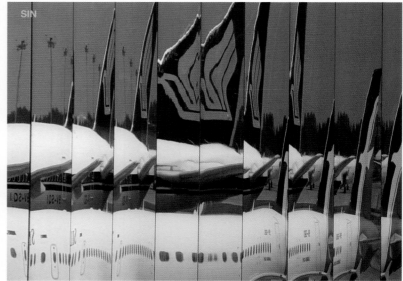

SIN

AMS

AMS

NRT

GLOSSARY OF KEY CONCEPTUAL TERMS/BIBLIOGRAPHY/AIRPORT CODES/ACKNOWLEDGMENTS

Glossary of key conceptual terms

Bare Life
For us, bare life is a term that describes the forms of life – from DNA coding to asylum seekers in detention centres – in which the body is opened directly to the working of politics. For more elaboration refer to Giorgio Agamben's *Homo Sacer*, and Michel Foucault's *Society Must be Defended*.

Biodigital Assemblage of Matter
This is a term we use to describe the increasingly complex body that one must become when travelling through an airport – part database identity, part baggage allowance, part biological body, part of a global machine of movement. The term does have more complex meanings that relate to the evolution of life. For further reading see Luciana Parisi's *Abstract Sex*.

Biometrics
This term refers quite literally to the 'measuring of life'. Biometrics encode unique bodily identifiers (such as thumb prints or retina patterns) into machine readable data. Biometrics are therefore non-transferable identification systems. For 'security reasons' they are being increasingly deployed and 'perfected' at airports.

Chronopolitics
Refers to the politics of time (Greek, *khronos*). The management of time is related to the politics of movement. The question of who and what moves and at what speed is therefore a crucial political issue. For more on this read Paul Virilio's and Sylvere Lotringer's *Pure War*.

Control Access Systems
Control access systems are becoming common in all forms of public life. Each time you swipe a card or enter a pin number in order to access a building, a phone, or an information network, you are using a control access system. These systems rely upon automated modes of pattern matching, rather than human systems of interpretation.

Control Society
This term signals a move in the operations of power in society from the methods of discipline and surveillance (where people willingly mould themselves into what they believe power requires them to be) to a society where people are controlled more directly through regulations and procedures. For more on this read Gilles Deleuze's "Postscript on Control Societies".

Haptics and Haptopolitics
Haptics relates to all the bodily senses of touch, such as air pressure on the skin, or the touch between various joints in the body. How a body is touched, and by whom or what, is a politically charged field. A new 'politics of touch' is being played out at the airport where many forms of biometrics require a direct touch of a body on a machine.

Heterotopia
A term borrowed from biology and ecology and developed by Michel Foucault in his essay "Of Other Spaces". In biology the term describes the displacement of an organ or other body part to an abnormal location. One could say that there is no set place for anything anymore – national security systems now exist side by side with shopping malls, airports themselves contain an increasing amount of services and functions that were once scattered across the city.

Information Architecture
Information architecture refers to the structures that facilitate the constant circulation of data, people, things and ideas. At the airport, we can clearly see how the structures of information management and urban planning are converging. [See Metastable Forms, Topological Architecture, Network Thinking.]

Metastable Forms

Airports are metastable, which is to say that they are stable in their constant instability.

Motion Capture

Usually relates to the optical technologies through which images of movement are captured, as in photography and cinematography. At the airport, motion capture has a more material articulation. Airports work to control movement by 'capturing', coding and directly manipulating the direction, pace and rhythm of all things that move through it. By using the term motion capture to describe both images and actions of motion, we want to signal the drift that is occurring in technical methods of mediation from 'representation' to 'regulation'.

Network thinking

Airports are nodes in the interconnected and overlapping global networks of transport, security, trade, travel, design and franchising (to name a few). All networks are based on relationships. Network thinking privileges the relations between objects rather than 'objects' themselves. When thinking about networks one tends to think about the connections, processes and procedures that enable things to link and associate with each other. All networks have political as well as technical dimensions. [See Topological Architecture, Non-places.]

Non-places

A term coined by Marc Augé in *Non-places: An Introduction to an Anthropology of Supermodernity*. Non-places are most clearly understood by looking at airports, shopping malls, highway systems or any spaces of transit where ones' relationship to the space is mediated through signs. Non-places are spaces that could be any place.

Nomos

A term that refers to a sovereign province. Derived from the ancient Greek term "nomos", for distributing and dividing, a nomos is a province with its own distinct sovereign structures – its own god, capital and frontiers.

Space of Flows

In a world of global movement, the flow of bodies, information and money is changing the rules of what defines territory, space and identity. New regulations of flow are also fundamentally changing the operations of global power. [For further reading see Manuel Castells, *The Information Age: Economy, Society and Culture*].

Terraforming

Quite literally the making of land. It is a common trope in science fiction and airport construction. Many new airports are being built on engineered islands made on totally reclaimed land. Terraforming is also suggestive of the possibilities of creating new worlds.

Topological Architecture

Networks create infrastructures that connect bodies, buildings and political institutions. The strict packeting of bodies and information in airports and information networks could be thought of as a form of topological architecture, inasmuch as they are structures that span fields normally thought of as discrete, by stitching a body into a building and a database. In this sense our use of the term also invokes the way in which contemporary architectural practice often uses computer modeling to give plasticity and malleability to architectural form. [See also Biometrics and Biodigital Assemblages of Matter.]

Bibliography

Agamben, Giorgio, *Means without End,* V Binetti and C Casarino trans, Minneapolis: University of Minnesota Press, 2000.

Agamben, Giorgio, *Homo Sacer: Sovereign Power and Bare Life,* Daniel Heller-Roazen trans, Stanford: Stanford University Press, 1998.

Augé, Marc, *Non-places: An Introduction to an Anthropology of Supermodernity*, J Howe trans, London: Verso, 1995.

Benjamin, Walter, *Illuminations*, Harry Zohn, trans, New York: Schocken, 1969.

Bergson, Henri, *Creative Evolution,* Arthur Mitchell trans, London: Dover Books, 1907.

Blankenship, Edward, *The Airport: architecture-urban intergration-ecological problems*, New York: Praeger Publishers 1974.

Blow, Christopher, *Airport Terminals*, Oxford: Butterworth-Heinemann, 1991.

Borja, J and Castells, M, "The impact of globalization on the spatial and social structure of cities", in *Local and Global: The Management of Cities in the Information Age*, EarthScan: New York, 1997

Brambilla, Marco, *Transit*, London: Booth-Clibborn Editions, 1999.

Bukatman, Scott, *Terminal Identity: The Virtual Subject in Postmodern Science Fiction*, Durham: Duke University Press, 1993.

Bukatman, Scott, "Zooming Out: The End of Offscreen Space", in *The New American Cinema,* Jon Lewis ed, Durham: Duke University Press, 1998.

Castells, Manuel, *The Information Age: Economy, Society and Culture,* Vols. 1-3, London: Blackwell, 1996.

Castells, Manuel, *The Rise of the Network Society*, Vol. 1, Oxford: Blackwell, 1998.

Coyne, Richard, *Technoromanticism: Digital Narrative, Holism And The Romance Of The Real*, Cambridge: MIT Press, 1999.

De Certeau, Michel, *The Practice of Everyday Life*, Steven Rendall trans, Berkeley: University of California Press, 1984.

Deleuze, Gilles and Guattari, Felix, *A Thousand Plateaus: Capitalism and Schizophrenia*, Brian Massumi trans, London: The Athlone Press, 1987.

Deleuze, Gilles, "Postscript on Control Societies", in *Negotiations*, New York: Columbia University Press,1995, pp. 169-183.

Edwards, Brian, *The Modern Terminal: New Approaches to Airport Architecture,* London: E & FN Spon, 1998.

Foucault Michel, "Of Other Spaces", *Diacritics,* Vol. 16, No. 1, 1986, pp. 22-27. Foucault, Michel, "Seminar of 17 March 1976", in *Society Must be Defended* New York: Picador, 1996.

Friedberg, Anne, *Window Shopping: Cinema and the Postmodern*, Berkeley: University of California Press, 1993.

Fuller, Gillian, "The Arrow – Directional Semiotics: Wayfinding in Transit", *Social Semiotics*, Vol. 12, No. 3, 2002.

Fuller, Gillian, "Life in Transit: Between airport and camp", *Borderlands*, Vol. 2 No. 1, 2003.

Fuller, Gillian, "Perfect Match: Biometrics and Body Patterning in a Networked World", *Fibreculture*, Vol. 1 No. 1, 2003.

Guattari, Felix, *The Three Ecologies,* London: The Athlone Press, 2000.

Harley, Ross, "Roller Coaster Planet: Kinetic Experience in the Age of Mechanical Motion", *Convergence: The Journal of Research into New Media Technologies*, London: Vol. 6, No. 3, Summer, 2000.

Harley, Ross, *Videoworks Double DVD*, Sydney: MediaComPress in association with the Museum of Contemporary Art, Sydney, 2003.

Hart, Walter, *The Airport Passenger Terminal*, New York: Wiley-Interscience Publication, 1985.

Hayles, Katherine, *How We Became Post Human: Virtual Bodies In Cybernetics, Literature, and Informatics*, Chicago: University of Chicago Press, 1999.

Hoete, Anthony, *ROAM: Reader on the Aesthetics of Mobility*, London: Black Dog Publising, 2003.

Horonjeff, Robert and McKelvey, Francis, *Planning and Design of Airports*, New York: McGraw-Hill, 1994.

Houben, Francine and Calabrese, Luisa Maria, *Mobility: A Room with a View*, Rotterdam: NAi Publishers, 2003.

Ibelings, Hans, *Supermodernism: Architecture in the Age of Globalisation*, Rotterdam: NAi Publishers, 2002.

International Civil Aviation Organisation Journal, *Annual Report*, Vol. 55, No. 6, July/August, 2000.

Iyer, Pico, *The Global Soul: Jet Lag, Shopping Malls, and the Search for Home*, New York: Vintage Books, 2000.

Kirby, Lynne, *Parallel Tracks: The Railroad and Silent Cinema*, Durham: Duke University Press, 1997.

Koolhaas, Rem et al, *Mutations: Harvard Project on the City*, Barcelona: Actar, 2001.

Koolhaas, Rem et al, *Great Leap Forward: Harvard Project on the City 1*, New York: Taschen, 2001.

Koolhaas, Rem et al, *Guide to Shopping: Harvard Project on the City 2*, New York: Taschen, 2001.

Kroker, Arthur, "The Image Matrix", *CTHEORY*, www.ctheory.net, 3/20/2002.

Latour, Bruno, *Aramis or The Love Of Technology*, Cambridge: Harvard University Press, 1999.

Lévy, Pierre, *Becoming Virtual: Reality in the Digital Age*, Robert Bononno trans, New York: Plenum Trade, 1998.

Lewis, William, *Airlines Executives and Federal Regulation; case studies in American enterprise from the airmail era to the dawn of the jet age*, Columbus: Ohio State University Press, 2000.

Massumi, Brian, *Parables for the Virtual: Movement, Affect, Sensation*, Durham: Duke University Press, 2002.

McLuhan, Marshall, *Understanding Media*, London: Abacus, 1964.

Morse, Margaret, *Virtualities*, Durham: Duke University Press, 1999.

Parisi, Luciana, *Abstract Sex: Philosophy, Biotechnology and the Mutations of Desire*, London: Continuum, 2004.

Pascoe, David, *Airspaces*, London: Reaktion Books, 2001.

Pawley, Martin, *Terminal Architecture*, London: Reaktion Books, 1998.

Penz, Francois and Thomas, Maureen, *Cinema and Architecture: Melies, Mallet-Stevens, Multimedia*, London: British Film Institute, 1997.

Pratchett, Terry, *Strata*, London: Corgi, 1988.

Rosler, Martha, *In the Place of the Public: Observations of a Frequent Flyer*, Frankfurt: Cantz Verlag, 1998.

Schivelbusch, Wolfgang, *The Railway Journey: The Industrialisation of Time and Space in the Nineteenth Century*, New York: Berg Publishers, 1977.

Serres, Michel, *Angels: a Modern Myth*, Paris: Flammarion, 1995.

Shaviro, Steven, *Connected: What it Means to Live in the Network Society*, Minneapolis: University of Minnesota Press, 2003.

Sorkin, Michael, *Variations on a Theme Park: The New American City and the End of Public Space*, New York: Noonday Press, 1992.

Stengers, Isabelle, "Whitehead and the Laws of Nature", in *Salzburger Theologische Zeitschrift*, 3 Issue 2, 1999, pp 193-206.

Stephenson, Neal, *The Diamond Age*, London: Bantam, 2000.

Sudjic, Deyan, *The Hundred Mile City*, London: Flamingo, 1993.

Taussig, Michael, "Miasma", in Gay Hawkins and Steven Muecke eds, *Culture and Waste*, Maryland: Rowman & Littlefield, 2003.

Taylor, Mark, "Terminal Space", in *Anywhere*, Cynthia Davidson ed, New York: Rizzoli, 1992.

Virilio, Paul and Lotringer, Sylvere, *Pure War,* New York: Semiotext(e) 1983.
Virilio, Paul, *The Aesthetics of Disappearance*, New York: Semiotext(e), 1991.

Virilio, Paul, *Open Sky*, Julie Rose trans, London: Verso, 1997.

Wark, McKenzie, *Virtual Geography: Living With Global Media*, Bloomington: Indiana University Press, 1994.

Wolfe, Cary, *Critical Environments: Postmodern Theory and the Pragmatics of the 'Outside'*, Minneapolis: Minnesota University Press,1998.

Airport Codes

An airport code is an UPPER CASE three-letter acronym (TLA) used to identify a specific airport. TLAs exist in many fields as they are useful for standardising and coding distinct objects – such as operating systems, (GNU, DOS), corporations (IBM, CNN) and computer application file extensions (JPG, EXE). In the case of airports, TLAs are assigned by IATA (the International Air Transport Association). There are approximately 9,000 in use of a total of 17,576 available. The database of available codes is constantly upgraded as new airports are built and others become obsolete.

The following 100 codes represent some of the major hubs and smaller nodes that, together, could be seen to constitute an alternative geography of a networked world.

*coded bold are documented in this book.

ADD	ADDIS ABABA	ETHIOPIA
AMS	**AMSTERDAM SCHIPHOL**	**THE NETHERLANDS**
ANR	ANTWERP	BELGIUM
ARN	STOCKHOLM ARLANDA	SWEDEN
BCN	BARCELONA	SPAIN
BEY	BEIRUT	LEBABON
BGW	BAGHDAD AL MUTHANA	IRAQ
BHO	BHOPAL	INDIA
BHX	BIRMINGHAM INTL	GREAT BRITAIN
BII	BIKINI ATOLL	MARSHALL ISLANDS
BIN	BAMIYAN	AFGHANISTAN
BKK	BANGKOK INT'L	THAILAND
BNE	**BRISBANE**	**AUSTRALIA**
BOG	BOGOTA	COLOMBIA
BOM	BOMBAY	INDIA
CAI	CAIRO	EGYPT
CBR	CANBERRA	AUSTRALIA
CCS	CARACAS	VENEZUELA
CDG	PARIS DE GAULLE	FRANCE
CHC	CHRISTCHURCH INTL	NEW ZEALAND (AOTEAROA)
CMN	CASABLANCA	MOROCCO
CNW	WACO(TX)	UNITED STATES
CPH	COPENHAGEN	DENMARK
DAM	DAMASCUS	SYRIA
DCA	WASHINGTON NATIONAL	UNITED STATES
DPS	DENPASAR	INDONESIA
DXB	DUBAI	UNITED ARAB EMIRATES
EWR	NEW YORK NY/ NEWARK INL	UNITED STATES
FCO	ROME	ITALY
FLG	FLAGSTAFF	UNITED STATES
FNA	FREETOWN LUNGI INTL	SIERRA LEONE
FOC	FUZHOU	CHINA
FRA	**FRANKFURT INTL**	**GERMANY**
HAM	HAMBURG	GERMANY

HAV	HAVANA	CUBA
HDD	HYDERABAD	PAKISTAN
HEL	HELSINKI VANTAA	FINLAND
HGH	HANGZHOU	CHINA
HIJ	HIROSHIMA	JAPAN
HKG	HONG KONG INTL	HONG KONG
HKT	PHUKET INTL	THAILAND
HLA	JOHANNESBURG	SOUTH AFRICA
HND	TOKYO HANEDA	JAPAN
HNL	HONOLULU INTL	UNITED STATES
HRE	HARARE	ZIMBABWE
IAD	**WASHINGTON DULLES**	**UNITED STATES**
JFK	**NEW YORK NY/ KENNEDY**	**UNITED STATES**
JKL	JACKSON KY	UNITED STATES
JKT	JAKARTA SOEKARNO	INDONESIA
JTR	SANTORINI	GREECE
JXN	JACKSON MI	UNITED STATES
KIX	**OSAKA KANSAI**	**JAPAN**
LAS	LAS VEGAS MCCARRAN	UNITED STATES
LAX	**LOS ANGELES INTL**	**UNITED STATES**
LGA	NEW YORK NY/LA GUARDIA	UNITED STATES
LGW	LONDON GATWICK	GREAT BRITAIN
LHR	**LONDON HEATHROW**	**GREAT BRITAIN**
LTN	LONDON LUTON INTL	GREAT BRITAIN
MDW	CHICAGO MIDWAY	UNITED STATES
MIA	**MIAMI**	**UNITED STATES**
MJQ	JACKSON MN	UNITED STATES
MKL	JACKSON TN	UNITED STATES
MSP	**MINNEAPOLIS/STPAUL**	**UNITED STATES**
NAS	NASSAU INTL	BAHAMAS
NCE	NICE COTE DAZUR	FRANCE
NRT	**TOKYO NARITA**	**JAPAN**
NUE	NUREMBERG	GERMANY
ORD	**CHICAGO O'HARE**	**UNITED STATES**

ORY	PARIS ORLY	FRANCE
OSL	OSLO	NORWAY
PHX	PHOENIX	UNITED STATES
PLZ	PORT ELIZABETH	SOUTH AFRICA
PNH	PHNOM PENH	CAMBODIA
PPT	PAPEETE FAAA	FRENCH POLYNESIA
PSY	PORT STANLEY	FALKLAND ISLANDS (MALVINAS)
PTY	PANAMA CITY INTL	PANAMA
PVG	**PUDONG**	**CHINA**
QND	NOVI SAD	YUGOSLAVIA
RAB	RABAUL	PAPUA NEW GUINEA
SAL	SAN SALVADOR INTL	EL SALVADOR
SCL	SANTIAGO	CHILE
SHA	SHANGHAI	CHINA
SIN	**SINGAPORE CHANGI**	**SINGAPORE**
SJJ	SARAJEVO	BOSNIA AND HERZEGOVINA
SJU	SAN JUAN MARIN INTL	PUERTO RICO
SKD	SAMARKAND	UZBEKISTAN
STN	LONDON STANSTED	GREAT BRITAIN
SYD	**SYDNEY**	**AUSTRALIA**
SZG	SALZBURG	AUSTRIA
TBS	TBILISI ALEXEYEVKA	GEORGIA
TFN	TENERIFE N LOSRODEO	SPAIN
THF	BERLIN TEMPELHOF	GERMANY
TLV	TEL AVIV-YAFO BEN GURION	ISRAEL
TPE	TAIPEI SHEK	TAIWAN
TUN	TUNIS CARTHAGE	TUNISIA
VSF	SPRINGFIELD	UNITED STATES
WAW	WARSAW	POLAND
YBA	BANFF	CANADA
YHZ	HALIFAX INTL	CANADA
YYZ	TORONTO	CANADA

Acknowledgments

Aviopolis is a multimedia project that would not exist without the assistance and participation of a great many people and organisations. In particular, we would like to thank Julie Miller, Philip Bell and all of the staff and students at the School of Media and Communications at the University of New South Wales for their interest, enthusiasm and support for the project. We are especially indebted to the design and packaging work done by Peter Cossey and Adnan Lalani over the past three years. Without them there would be no website or CD-ROM or info-graphics. We would also like to thank Morgan Richards, our researcher in the early stages of the project: we are still working through all the archival material she found. The Faculty of Arts and Social Sciences at UNSW has supported our work by way of a number of research grants which enabled us to get the project off the ground. We are also grateful to Ted Kleiner and Greg Trevor at the Port Authority of New York and New Jersey for providing their time and access to archival materials relating to JFK International Airport. Thanks must also go to Karen Harrigan and her staff at Sydney Airports Corporation, who generously granted us access to film landside and airside facilities (a big thank you in particular to Joe Rewa, John Stone and all the guys at Operations). David Holm at Woodhead International gave us great insight into current architectural issues and introduced us to the airport boom in China. We would also like to thank the Cultural Studies/Comparative Literature crew at the FlightTime conference, University of Minnesota, March 2002, for the opportunity to present an early version of our work on airport semiology and wayfinding; and to the organisers of the Security Bytes conference, University of Lancaster, July 2004, for the chance to talk biometrics and politics of fear. We are also grateful to those who have shown and published earlier iterations of this project: *Digital Biedermeier*, Vienna, 2002; *Imaging the City*, Museum of Contemporary Art, Sydney, 2003; *Social Semiotics*; *Borderlands ejournal*; and *Fibreculture Journal*. We would like to thank all participants at the Biophilosophy Residency, ANU in September 2003, organised by Brian Massumi, Sandra Buckley and Stephen Zagala: an exercise in translogic that worked. Conversations with Anna Munster, Chris Chesher, Manuel De Landa, Gay Hawkins, and Lev Manovich have challenged and inspired us in many ways. Thanks to Sandy Wagner for all her work and Chris O'Hanlon for the introduction. We would also like to thank Gavin Ambrose, Duncan McCorquodale and the staff at BDP for their contribution to the shape and form of the book. And last of all, a big thank you to the man in the office next door, Andrew Murphie, who always suggests exactly the right reading at the right time.

Aviopolis A book about airports
© 2004 Black Dog Publishing Limited
All rights reserved
Aviopolis multimedia concept by Fuller + Harley
Photography by Ross Rudesch Harley
Text by Gillian Fuller
Designed by Gavin Ambrose
Infographics/illustration by Peter Cossey and Adnan Lalani
www.aviopolis.com

Architecture Art Design
Fashion History Photography Theory and Things

Black Dog Publishing Limited
Unit 4.4 Tea Building
56 Shoreditch High Street
London E1 6JJ UK
T 44 020 7613 1922 F 44 020 7613 1944
E info@bdp.demon.co.uk www.bdpworld.com

British Library Cataloguing-in-Publication Data.
A catalogue record for this book is available from the British Library.
ISBN 1 904772 11 0